WHAT EVERY COLLEGE
STUDENT SHOULD KNOW

WHAT EVERY COLLEGE STUDENT SHOULD KNOW

How to Find the Best Teachers and Learn the Most from Them

ERNIE LEPORE AND SARAH-JANE LESLIE

Rutgers University Press   *New Brunswick, New Jersey*

Third paperback printing, 2002

Library of Congress Cataloging-in-Publication Data
LePore, Ernest, 1950–
    What every college student should know : how to find the best
    teachers and learn the most from them / Ernie Lepore and Sarah-Jane
    Leslie.
        p. cm.
        ISBN 0-8135-3066-0 (alk. paper)
        1. College teaching. 2. College teachers. 3. College student
    orientation. I. Leslie, Sarah-Jane, 1981– II. Title.

LB2331 .L4 2002
378.1'2—dc21

                                                            2001048397

British Cataloging-in-Publication data for this book is available from the
British Library.

Manufactured in the United States of America

Contents

Acknowledgments

We are indebted to many people for their input and help with this book. For providing that essential undergraduate perspective, we would like to thank Alison Gibbs, Leeann Fecho, Erica Fields, Yvelisse Suarez, and, in particular, Seth Cable and Nadia Salim. For advice and feedback on academic issues, we are indebted to Justine Hernandez, Stephen Herman, and especially Peter Klein. We would also like to thank Marlie Wasserman for her support and Marilyn Campbell for her extremely helpful editorial comments. And, finally, Sarah-Jane would like thank Alan, Joan, and Rachel Leslie for all their generosity, patience, and support.

WHAT EVERY COLLEGE STUDENT SHOULD KNOW

Introduction
Why Students Need This Book

College years are full of hopes. You want to succeed academically and finish up with a great transcript and résumé. You want to take terrific classes with inspirational teachers. And, of course, you want to enjoy your college years, balancing study with friends and fun. Many students settle for less, but why should you?

It's easy to drift passively through your college career, but that means losing out on rewarding experiences and opportunities. Why should you settle for whatever professor you happen to end up with, especially if this professor can't teach and puts you to sleep every time he opens his mouth? Why should you sit overlooked and undervalued in his classroom? And why should you end up with a set of lukewarm recommendations after four years of hard work?

College is fraught with pitfalls, and even with the best intentions, it's hard to avoid them.

The first step toward getting the most out of your college education is to learn how to find your school's best teachers. In high school, students have little or no flexibility when selecting teachers and courses. Many entering students assume that colleges work the same way. Luckily, college students have a lot of freedom to pick and choose. Students are rarely *forced* to settle for lousy professors—as long as they are willing to look for the good ones and know how to do so.

Once you've found a great professor, you need to figure out what she expects from her students, and how you can best get to know her and let her get to know *you*. Building relationships with professors is one of the most important and most overlooked aspects of a great college career. Professors are often the best sources of opportunities, advice, and support. Having them on your side can make all the difference between a mediocre college career and a terrific one.

Relationships with professors start in the classroom. In most classes, the professor gets to know only a few students. These students receive most of his attention. They are much more likely than the other students are to receive the support they need to do well in his course. Because the teacher interacts with these students more than with the rest of the class, his lectures also become more geared toward them. He may well even take greater time and care in grading their work and giving feedback. Ultimately, these students end up learning more from the professor than the rest of the class does. You need to make sure you're one of those students.

The next step toward building a relationship lies outside the lecture hall. You might feel awkward or shy about talking one-on-one with your instructor. Some students avoid office hours as a result. Even if they do visit, they're often unprepared and so don't get the help they need. However, if these meetings are handled right, they can be very beneficial and may lead to further opportunities such as independent study and research projects, which add another dimension to your college education.

Once the semester ends, students often put their courses behind them, and never even find out their grades on the final exams or projects. But giving up so quickly can leave you with lower grades than you deserve. The grading process leaves a lot more room for error than most students realize. Perhaps the professor didn't read your answers carefully, or perhaps she simply wrote the grade down incorrectly (which happens more than you might think). Abandoning final assignments also leaves students without feedback they could have learned from. A visit after the final gets you this deserved feedback and protects you against grading inaccuracies.

After spending four years working hard to get a great education, students deserve letters of recommendation that reflect what they've accomplished. Sadly, though, they often end up with recommendations that are clichéd and uninformative. Every year countless candidates for graduate and professional schools are rejected because they handed in weak or inappropriate recommendations. Getting superior evaluations can be tricky, but it's well worth the effort. After all, future careers often hang on no more than a couple of recommendations.

Ultimately, the college experience you have is up to you. You can settle for poor teachers, poor guidance, and poor recommendations—but you don't have to. All you need to get the most out of your college education is a proactive attitude and a little guidance; if you've got the attitude, we'll provide the advice.

1 Before Classes Begin
Finding Good Teachers

Each semester students register for classes without knowing anything about the people who will be teaching them. Rising tuition, heavy course loads, and long semesters merit more informed choices, but university curricula, especially in the first two years, are full of requirements, and students often figure that it doesn't matter who's doing the teaching. "Take the class and complete the requirement!" But it matters who is teaching. It matters a lot.

Imagine yourself, uncertain about your career plans, taking a required course whose subject matter is completely foreign to you—not an uncommon situation. Your first encounter with the subject may be your last. Discarding a discipline just because an uninformed choice landed you with an uninspiring teacher may be a great loss—a loss an informed choice might have prevented. Even if a requirement is your only taste of a field, it shouldn't be a trial. Good teachers stimulate interest. Your intended major, or even your career plans, could easily change because you fall in love with a subject. (In fact, one of the authors had no idea what she wanted to major in when she entered college. A string of great professors led her to a major she would never have predicted.)

These opportunities are too often lost because of poor teaching. Of course, you might not be in the market for new subjects, but it's still worth your while to find good professors. Though you (and your parents) remain certain that your destiny lies in medicine or law or business, why should you undervalue your time? Why should so many hours be wasted and boring, or, even worse, painful and exhausting? By picking an inspiring teacher, you'll enjoy your courses as much as the student who takes only courses that appeal to him will.

The question is how to find the right teacher. This task isn't an easy one, but it can be done, and success is well rewarded. But before we get to strategies, let's briefly examine other factors that should figure into your class selection.

Subject Matter

Subject matter would seem to be the primary reason for choosing a course, but it can be overrated. Though it must be a consideration, it shouldn't be the final word on course selection. When the teaching is poor, an appealing subject matter won't make much difference, but good teaching can inspire unexpected interest. Every year students discover and enjoy topics they knew nothing about before their classes began. Some students even enroll in courses exclusively on the basis of the teacher's good reputation. An excellent teacher is unlikely to teach a boring class; good teachers can breathe interest into just about any subject.

We're not telling you to major in Good Teachers (although individualized majors *are* fashionable these days); rather we want to emphasize their significance to you. In high school probably you didn't get to pick and choose who taught you. You chose subjects and were assigned teachers. But not in college. In most colleges, especially in introductory classes and required courses, you often have a choice among instructors. Whenever possible, take advantage of this choice.

Scheduling Considerations

The purpose of finding quality teaching is to let you get the most out of the course. But great teachers aside, you're still going to have to attend class. A competent professor will give you a powerful incentive to attend, which is among the best reasons for finding one. But as you're choosing, don't dismiss scheduling considerations. If, for example, you know you're not the sort of person to get up for an eight a.m. class, registering for one is a pretty lousy idea. Of course, if it's a toss-up between a terrific professor early in the morning or a useless one later in the day, invest in a coffeemaker and haul yourself out of bed. But if the professors aren't so different, then why take a class you're sure to cut?

The importance of the class also needs to be considered. If you're trying out a new subject—one that is perhaps an untested candidate for your major—then it's worth doing everything you can do to land in the classroom of the best instructor. Wouldn't it be sad to dismiss a field you might have enjoyed just because you got a poor teacher early on? If that legendary prof teaches only at dawn or on Friday afternoon, make the sacrifice.

A Background Check

Okay. So you're pumped up, ready to find your good teacher. But how do you find out if a teacher's worth taking? You have several available options.

Asking Around

Suppose you're considering a particular class. Your first step should be to find out the instructor's name. Although you can go through an entire course without learning the professor's name—as happens at an alarming rate—we suggest that you don't even register without knowing it. Finding an instructor's name is usually easy, but sometimes a name is not immediately available when you register. Sometimes the instructor's name may not appear in the course catalogue or whatever other registration document is used at your college. If it isn't, the department that is offering the course will know who will be teaching it. Contact someone there and find out. (One of us only recently realized she could do this. It saves a *lot* of hassle.)

Once you've found out your instructor's name, gathering information about him or her is easier if you're a returning student, and still do-able if you're an entering freshman or a transfer student. Former students can vouch for a teacher's ability. Of course, you may not know any of these students straight off, but they won't be too hard to find. When balanced against the time-investment that a course requires, finding a friend-of-a-friend is worth the effort. However, your information is only as good as its source. Students can often be unreliable judges. If their information seems questionable, move on.

Graduate students often prove invaluable. They are more knowledgeable than undergraduates about a professor's competence. They're also likely to be honest, especially if you promise confidentiality. The next best bet is another professor, or your advisor if you have one. Your advisor may only be able to give you limited help, though, unless she is from the relevant department. Most faculty and administrative staff at large institutions are unfamiliar with people outside their own fields. Finding someone in the right discipline can help. Although professors have much to lose by denouncing a colleague's teaching skills, it's almost impossible for them to withhold judgment. There's no shortage of loose lips in universities! Listen carefully to what they say; their honest opinion lurks not far beneath the surface of their words, even as they're exclaiming that they cannot make such assessments. (For one thing, ask yourself when they're more likely to protest that they can't make such a judgment call: if they think the teacher is great, or if they think he's awful. Which would *you* avoid saying?) These subtle assessments are great guides to choosing a professor. Collect as many opinions as you can.

An easy way for you to get a professor's opinion without putting her on the spot is to present her with a list of possible teachers. Could she recommend to you anyone on the list? Which would be the best section? This lets her subtly ignore poor colleagues without explicitly putting them down. If you aren't familiar with the professor you are asking, steer clear of questions that would require her to bad-mouth her colleagues. Students are a better source of negative information.

Student Evaluations of Teachers

Near the end of each term, teachers are usually evaluated by their students. Most teachers learn little from these evaluations, and it's unclear just who is supposed to profit from them and how. Common wisdom is that they are essential for professional promotions (see the Afterword), but you'd have a hard time finding anyone who was denied promotion merely because she received poor teaching evaluations. (At least at large institutions; in this regard smaller institutions are way ahead of the pack.) The hope of most administrations is that these student evaluations will help your professors become better teachers, which is a very good aim. But the questions asked in these evaluations are usually vague and unspecific. In many institutions your evaluations either disappear or lie unexamined once a term ends.

Evaluations are not to be trusted unconditionally, but if you can get your hands on them, they can be a useful source of information. Consulting them might give you an idea of a teacher's abilities. In many institutions evaluations are available for student review, although few students take advantage of the opportunity. (The library is a good starting point if you don't know where to look for them, or you might try asking the department directly if they can make past student evaluations available to you.) Take advantage of this resource and look over the impressions of fellow students of previous classes. Profit from your predecessors' misery!

The First Few Classes

Most colleges afford students the chance to add and drop classes once a term begins. Information on procedures (deadlines, required signatures, etc.) shouldn't be difficult to obtain, if you don't have it already. Check registration web sites, and any course lists and handouts you have. Much of this material should also be in your college's catalogue, which you should obtain as soon as you arrive on campus, if it is not already in your preregistration packet. Upperclassmen and faculty advisors can also help you.

Once you have the add-and-drop dates, mark them on your calendar. Missing the deadlines can mean your being stuck in an undesirable class for a whole semester. Assuming you have add/drop options, attending the first few class meetings can provide you with a terrific overview of a professor and her course. If you like what you see and hear, stay enrolled; if you don't, drop the course. Shop around! If a course has multiple sections, register for one but check out the others. This option allows you to decide for yourself whether an instructor is any good.

Of course, time constraints limit your attending every possible course. As a note of caution, it's hard to catch up if you miss the first week or so of a class. Attend *all* the possible sections and courses you might want to take. This trial period should last only for a few busy days. It's much better than trying out one section one week and another the next. Make your decisions as quickly as you can before classes become full. To be able to act quickly, you need to do your research beforehand. Use evaluations and former students to narrow down your list, but don't make a final decision until you've seen the instructor in action.

What Makes for Good Teaching?

Before deciding on a course, and even before heading off for the first trial lecture, you should have some idea of what you're looking for. The same goes for when you're canvassing the opinions of former students. You may value many qualities in a teacher, some more than others. Here are the most important features to look for and—where possible—how you can discern them from a lecture or two or from former students' comments.

Preparation

Look for good preparation. You may learn in the course of your investigations that a teacher is well organized: students know in advance what to read; materials assigned are discussed as scheduled; discussions are focused; written assignments are returned within a reasonable amount of time; tests and papers are assigned with sufficient notice. A prepared teacher will aim to do all these things consistently.

The first day of class holds invaluable clues. Does the professor walk in, tell you what books to buy, and then summarily dismiss the class? A teacher should be prepared on the very first day to introduce her subject matter. If her attitude toward the first class is cavalier, drop the class. (Rumor has it that a professor at our university once walked in, chugged a beer, belched, then started teaching. Not a good sign.) Teachers, like students, may or may not be excited about the beginning of a new semester. If your prospective teacher shows neither vim nor vigor, she's unlikely to develop enthusiasm later. So unless you have a great reason to think she's basically a good teacher having an off day, find someone else.

The Syllabus

One simple but excellent telltale sign of preparation is whether the teacher begins the course by distributing a syllabus. If the teacher lacks the desire or energy to prepare a syllabus, how likely is he to be prepared for each class meeting? If he does provide a syllabus, look to see what's on it. Does it include his name (and his teaching assistants' names, if there are any)? Does he list a course calendar, including reading assignments, lecture topics, the dates on which quizzes will be given and papers will be due? Required texts? Supplementary texts? Has he ordered books, or placed them on reserve in the library? Has he checked to see whether the required texts are in the bookstore? Does his syllabus indicate what his course objectives and grading procedures are? His office hours? Office phone numbers and e-mail addresses? Has he set up a home page for his course?

The right answers to these questions show that a teacher has thought seriously about his course, and his students' needs, and he is sufficiently prepared to have made a plan. The calendar (usually included in the syllabus) carries real advantages for a student: it fosters quality preparation. If you know in advance what a teacher will be talking about on Monday and you know which readings are relevant to that topic, then you can prepare. However, if a teacher keeps his discussion topics secret, it's much harder to be ready for class.

Information about his grading policies is also important. Many students are deeply concerned about grades (as well they should be—see Chapter 4) and want to know precisely how their final grades will be determined. Do all of the quizzes count equally? What's the attendance policy? Is attendance required? Will there be a final exam? Are there opportunities for makeup exams? These are all reasonable questions. You have a right to expect answers at the outset of a course.

In short, you can find out a great deal about the carefulness, concern, and clarity of a professor by carefully examining her syllabus. If her syllabus leaves key questions unanswered, ask about them in class at the very first meeting. Attend to what sort of response you receive. Are her answers satisfactory? Remember you're not just getting answers. You are auditioning this person as a prospective teacher. The fact that you don't know her grading policies immediately is not the issue. The real issue is whether this innocent enough gap may reflect a deeper and more problematic lack of organization or interest on her part. If she hasn't taken the time to plan out the course—or if she doesn't care enough to let her students know her plans—she may be an indifferent teacher.

Interest and Excitement

How vital is the teacher's interest or enthusiasm? Are interesting or exciting teachers always effective? Sometimes students consider a teacher interesting because he has a hardy supply of jokes, great classroom rapport, or a friendly personality. Although you shouldn't play down these qualities, you mustn't overemphasize them either. Flair, spark, and verve are no substitutes for clarity, labor, and dedication. If his lectures lack substance, attending them will be a waste of your time. We aren't telling you to rush to the opposite extreme. A teacher with a dry, monotone voice will not hold your attention. If he puts you to sleep, you're probably not learning much. Of course, it's often not an either-or situation. A balance is ideal— the best teachers are both engaging and focused on their subject matter.

Flexibility

Although professors shouldn't gear their lectures to the worst students in their classes, they should be ready to change their schedules to accommodate their audience. A teacher should determine early in the term how knowledgeable students are and quickly adjust his pace and program. Teachers who involve the class on the first few days will have a better idea of how prepared their students are. Some teachers set their sights too low, some too high. Students vary from term to term, so last term's pace needn't coincide with the current one. Some may even ask about prior courses—an excellent indication of a flexible teacher. Amassing this sort of information helps a professor adjust the level of his lectures and assignments. A teacher who walks in and lectures without paying any attention to student involvement is most likely inflexible. His level of interaction is key here. If his course resembles a spectator sport, then he probably has little interest in accommodating your abilities.

Professional Accomplishments

Students often hear about their teacher's accomplishments: published books, honors bestowed. But do these sorts of factors correlate at all with good teaching? Professional accomplishment often indicates intellectual enthusiasm, which is an advantage in the classroom. The teacher may be able to answer questions more quickly and accurately. If she has done a lot of research in her field, she may also be able to give deeper perspectives to her lectures. Her own interest in the subject will probably shine through and be inspirational. As a bonus, an accomplished professor's recommendation for admission into a professional school or graduate program will undoubtedly count for more than, say, a young, uncelebrated graduate student's. (More on this in Chapter 5.) Professional accomplishment isn't the final word in good teaching but it's certainly a plus.

In regard to finding accomplished faculty, here's an interesting tidbit for you to keep in mind. Many of the best undergraduate colleges impose such heavy teaching demands on their faculty members that they have little time for research and other duties. As a result, the most competitive undergraduate programs don't always have the most professionally accomplished faculty. A professor's accomplishments generally come from his research, so naturally the most accomplished ones will go where they can devote the most time to this research. So never figure that your school can't have a terrific faculty just because it doesn't have one of the most prestigious departments in the field; great faculty may well be right under your nose. Keep your eyes open for these people as you are researching teachers. It's possible to receive a better education at a less prestigious school. Remember that many opportunities exist at every college; the trick is to find them and take advantage of them. Don't be passive.

Accessibility

Naturally, you want a teacher who keeps office hours and replies to e-mails or phone messages. But some professors don't do so reliably and others divert students to graduate assistants. Based on your prior research, have you learned whether your prospective teacher makes himself available to students? How are his office hours conducted? You want someone accommodating and professional.

Some teachers are just no good at interacting with students. They may be shy. They may be impatient. They may frustrate easily. Each of these factors is critical in determining whether to register for a course. Don't underestimate them. Chances are you will need the counsel and direction of the teacher during the course of a term, but if interactions with her are awkward, don't expect much help. Former students are an authority on this. They will have already gone through a term with her and can judge how patient, helpful, and approachable she is. Ask them specifically how available she makes herself. Relying on the first lecture is trickier in this case, but watch how well she interacts with your classmates. Does she create an open atmosphere by encouraging students to participate? Does she mention how to get in contact with her? Watch out for professors who discourage students from reaching them. (One of us remembers asking a professor when he would be on campus, and he replied on most Wednesday afternoons. Not a good sign.)

Feedback

You should expect feedback from your teachers. Have prior students told you whether this teacher comments on submitted work? How she responds to questions and whether she respects your needs should be examined carefully. Are old tests made available? Does she put them up on a home page for the course? If you've found a student who has taken her class, ask to look at old papers or exams she graded. What sort of comments do you find? Are number or letter grades distributed without explanation? Did she provide answer sheets? Ideally, the grader should make a note to show or explain where the student went wrong and what a correct response would have been. If profound conceptual problems (and not just an innocent typo or misremembered fact) underlie an incorrect answer, these should be addressed. She should also supply missing information if a given response was insufficient. A big red mark doesn't help you learn much. Watch out for unexplained X's and question marks. If your teacher doesn't take the time to grade informatively, that reflects a lack of respect for your work. You want someone who cares about how much work you have done and how much you have learned.

Expectations

Related to feedback is the question of how much the teacher expects from his students. Easy courses are certainly not always best. But sometimes less work is preferable, depending on your needs and prior commitments for that term. Early in the course, perhaps on the basis of the syllabus alone, you might be able to determine whether your teacher's expectations are right for you. The reading and writing required may be more than you can manage. If so, shop around until you find a course better suited to your needs. Or you may be looking for a challenge, and the course in question may not be demanding enough.

Giving Notes

Note taking is an important part of academic success since you will use your notes to study for tests. Some teachers give good notes. Others don't. Students will not be able to take good notes from the chalkboard if the teacher's boardwriting is atrocious. Does the teacher write big enough so that students at the back can see the words? Does the teacher of a large class or a teacher with obviously bad handwriting use an overhead projector, handouts, or PowerPoint? Are his projections or notes carefully prepared, easy to read, easy to follow? If the instructor turns his back and puts too much information on the blackboard, his teaching will probably become tedious, with lots of time wasted. (Maybe the professor is trying to eat up time. Filibustering is one form of bad teaching.) Using a projector or handouts solves these problems.

Summary

Knowledge, preparation, interest, feedback, and accessibility are qualities you should seek in a teacher. Information about these features is what you want, whether based on the opinions of past students or other professors or on a one-week preview. But you might wonder whether these standards are so high as to eliminate almost every teacher. Satisfying them all would make for a model teacher and model teachers, sadly enough, are rare. It would be bold but impractical not to settle for less. Possibly you won't find even one teacher who meets all these high standards. Good teaching is a matter of degree. Eliminate the worst and settle for the best of what's available. Implementing our evaluation process will undoubtedly let you find the best available teacher even if she isn't perfect.

At this point you may be wondering whether the sort of Herculean effort that we have been describing is necessary. Our answer is resoundingly yes! Few things in life are worse than enduring a term of pathetic teaching. We're trying to help you avoid bad teaching and give you your best shot at an exciting education. You mustn't suppose you're safe just because you are at a superior university or at a college avowedly devoted to teaching. No university or college can guarantee a wonderful experience in every class. All you can expect is for good teachers to be available at your school. It's up to you to find them.

Contingencies

Suppose you are stuck taking a required course from an inferior teacher. What can you do? Find out who else, if anyone, teaches the course that term. If a second instructor might be better, see if you can register for her section. At many institutions sections fill up before registration ends; once the term starts switching is impossible. Suppose the good teacher's section is closed. You may still be able to attend her lectures, although take your tests in the class you were assigned. A lot of room for creativity exists—use your imagination. Work something out, so that you can learn from the good teacher. Flattery is almost always irresistible. When you regale a faculty member with all the anecdotes you have heard from unnamed colleagues and prior students about his superior teaching, he'll want you in his class and often find a way to register you.

What if you should find out that only bad instructors are teaching the course this term? Check out whether only those professors ever teach the course. If not, see who else teaches it and when. Take the course another term, if you can. Granted, sometimes you just have to bite the bullet and settle for what was assigned to you. But survey all the possible selections before you bite anything!

But what are you to do if your research suggests that bad teachers always teach the course? In that case, there's little you can do. You have to work hard and try to learn despite lousy teaching. You can't choose not to take the course if the course is required. In this case, you need to become more self-educating in such a course. The lessons regarding self-education can carry over to all courses. Don't miss this opportunity. Still, the best you can do is minimize these instances during your undergraduate stint. Fortunately, only a few courses are taught only by awful professors. For the rest of the time, a little research goes a long way.

Conclusion

You shouldn't necessarily conclude that if you dislike someone's teaching that he or she is a bad teacher. The student-teacher relationship is, after all, a relationship. It takes two to tango. What's great for someone else may be awful for you and vice versa. There are, however, some measures that are helpful to most people. Take time to find out something about your prospective professors.

- ✔ Ask other faculty members or former students to evaluate the professor.
- ✔ Look up a previous class's evaluations, if available.
- ✔ Attend the first few lectures of a course.
- ✔ Look for a professor who is prepared, interested, organized, and dedicated.

Conduct the research as best you can, bearing in mind that, however long this task takes, the time investment is small in comparison to an entire term and wasted tuition dollars.

CASE STUDIES

David's Problem

David is a first-semester freshman and has no idea of how to work with the registration system at his college. He has no set plans for his major but is hoping to find some interesting courses. He has quite a few requirements to get out of the way as well. Most of them sound pretty boring but they are necessary.

David registered with other incoming freshmen using a different system from the upperclassmen. He didn't have a chance to choose sections, let alone teachers, but then again he never chose teachers in high school. Why should he expect college to be any different? The two classes he's most looking forward to are political science and anthropology. They sound like the sorts of topics that interest him, and he hopes he will enjoy them both.

The course that David is least excited about is freshman writing. He's heard a ton of college students complain about it, but most schools seem to require it. He is prepared to suffer through it but isn't enthusiastic.

The Solution

David needs to become acquainted with his school's registration system. He needs to learn about the add-drop deadline, and he needs to go to the registrar's office to ask for specifics on the process, the forms, and the fees. Although an incoming student may have little control over his schedule until he gets to college, once there he might discover that he has much room to maneuver. In this regard colleges are typically very different from high schools, where one is often simply stuck with a certain schedule. Once David learns the ropes for changing his schedule, he can use this information to ensure that he gets the best term he can. Either through talking to older students or through observing the first few classes, he can find out whether his teachers are worth sticking with. He should take special care with his anthropology and political science classes. It would be a tragedy if he were turned off the topics by poor instructors. As these are his first encounters with these subjects, he deserves an unobstructed view of them, not one clouded by poor teaching. There may be less he can do about his freshman writing class. Still, as all freshmen take the course, there will be many sections. With a little research he may be able to make the best of the situation, using add-drop options to change sections. The important thing is for him not to take a helpless and passive attitude toward his college schedule.

Alice's Problem

Alice grew up in a small town, where she attended the local high school and finished with only ninety-three other students in her graduating class. The idea of going to a college with a hundred times that number of students in her year was frightening, so she chose a small liberal arts college that promised individual attention and an intimate environment. The college has worked out well socially, but not academically.

On the whole the college has a fine reputation but that doesn't help Alice much. The problem is that she intends to be a clinical psychologist, but her school's psychology department is terrible. The department has only five professors, one of whom doesn't even teach courses. Now in her second year Alice is disappointed with her professors' teaching abilities. One is so disorganized that he managed to lose an entire class's exams. The others are not much better. Alice has started to hate taking classes in her major. She wishes she had looked into the specific department before choosing her college.

The Solution

Alice is right to regret not having researched her department, but it's too late to worry about past mistakes. Her problem is not locating a good psychology professor at her school, since it appears none exist. However, one may be *better* than the rest. In this case she would do well to take as many classes with him as possible. The worst teacher of the lot should, of course, be resolutely avoided.

She should also consider more radical measures. If she is happy socially, transferring may not be an appealing option, but it is nonetheless worth considering. If she had realized her predicament during her freshman year, that would have been a good time to act. A poor department can only mean that her interest in her major will dwindle, and she will probably not learn much in the end. Transferring to a college that offers an excellent psychology program will allow her to benefit from good teaching and other opportunities.

She might worry that she won't be as prepared as the other psychology students in the new college. In this case she should take summer classes at the new institution. As the first two years in most colleges are often devoted largely to general education requirements, transferring at this stage will probably not pose obstacles to completing her major in four years. She can find out more about this from the new college's web site, or consult their catalogue on transfer credits, or request more information over the phone. If she still has outstanding questions, the college will most likely have someone to talk to her about her concerns. The situation here is not so different from applying as a freshman.

Alice does have another more risky option open to her. She could talk to a dean or a faculty member in her department about the problem. She would need to be extremely frank, but it might open up new avenues for her. Most professors are only too happy to help eager students access more opportunities, such as lab work or independent study, and such personal attention could offset her poor classroom experiences. Of course, as her assessment of the department is less than flattering, she risks incurring resentment from small-minded faculty. Thus, she should be prepared to go ahead and transfer if this strategy fails, so as not to let her situation worsen.

If she decides to go ahead and talk to a faculty member, Alice needs to be careful about what she says. If there is a psychology professor who seems a bit better than the others, she should address him. He need not even be better as far as teaching goes, but could simply be one she could stand to work with or whom she thinks might be more willing to help her. When addressing him, she should avoid confrontational and accusatory statements. Thus instead of saying "This department sucks, man. You people can't teach" (or words to that effect), she should tell him that she feels that her needs aren't being met under her current circumstances. She would like to be learning more in her classes, and wishes there were more opportunities and options available to her. Could he please help her make more of her major?

Of course, Alice may choose not to pursue the above options. As she is already in her second year, transferring may not be a possibility she wishes to pursue if she is happy and settled socially, and indeed, maybe she should have acted earlier. We would recommend that she do so, but she may already be resolved to stay.

Changing majors would also be advisable, if Alice were not set on becoming a professional psychologist. With this in mind, she should take some time out to think carefully about whether she really wants to pursue this major. Sometimes dissatisfaction with the department might be misplaced. She might be finding that the subject is just not right for her. Assuming this is not the case, though, then as she is not in a position to change the first major, she might consider taking a second one—perhaps in a related field—that will let her take classes from more talented teachers. Even if she doggedly pursues a psychology major at her current institution, adding another major would give her a more balanced—and less painful!—education.

2 In the Classroom
Getting the Most out of Good Teachers

Lectures offer great opportunities for learning, but they are all too often wasted. You can easily get by in a course without worrying about your behavior in the lecture hall, but if your aim is more than getting by, your first step begins in the classroom. Pay close attention to the professor, not merely by listening to his words. Every professor brings different expectations to his classroom. Attuning yourself to what they are can help you a lot. Conversely, every professor responds well to some sorts of behavior and badly to others. Following a few basic strategies will enable you to get the most out of your time in the classroom.

The Good Student

Like any other craft teaching has diverse practitioners. Some instructors prefer lectures; others discussions. Some distribute notes; some use overhead projectors; some write on blackboards. Testing formats vary and grading policies differ. The way professors interact with students can also differ. No two teachers are exactly alike. And so students who resolve to be *good students,* period, are making a big mistake.

At least since nursery school you've been told what a good

student is and isn't supposed to do. How could you be expected to resist the idea that there's a formula for being a good student?

Given all that you have been told (by parents and teachers) you might resolve to enter each class with a raft of good intentions—from taking notes in class to reading everything assigned; from handing assignments in on time to studying well in advance. These are admirable ideals and nothing is wrong with pursuing them. But even if you do, will the blind pursuit of these goals actually result in the highest achievement possible?

Undoubtedly students who are attentive and prepared tend to do better than those who are not. But organization and determination aren't always enough. Teachers differ; your teacher will have her own expectations and practices. And, unlike standard high school curricula, at most colleges and universities, administrators do not dictate course content or teaching practices. The teacher herself decides what to cover, so not only teaching ability but also course content and requirements can vary greatly. Recognizing these sorts of differences can make a world of difference to what you need to do to succeed. To be a good student you must not only learn the subject matter; you must also understand your teacher's expectations.

A Teacher's Expectations

In the last chapter we discussed how to go about identifying good teachers. But even after having found one, you still have to figure out what his expectations are. Don't be lulled by preconceptions about what every good student must do.

Some students seem able to intuit their teachers' expectations. Sometimes a teacher's and a student's styles fortuitously coincide. The rest of us aren't so lucky. Often good intentions get thwarted because what you have resolved and what your teacher expects don't coincide.

We are not recommending sycophancy. Winning your teacher's fondness is not your goal here, and massaging your teacher isn't the best way to learn anatomy. Kissing up rarely achieves anything. "Know thy teacher" is our motto. The instructor can't adapt to every individual student; you need to learn your teacher's individual style and expectations and then adapt to them. Students sometimes break their backs preparing for classes and still wind up with poor grades because they worked to meet their own preconceived ideas rather than their teacher's actual expectations. If your instructor is concerned primarily with your capacity for problem solving, memorizing the textbook isn't going to be much help; it will only destroy your social life.

Listen carefully to whatever hints your professor drops about his expectations on the first few days of class. Be prepared to adjust your habits accordingly. Pay attention to the questions students ask and how your teacher answers them. The first quiz or paper can also give indications. Accommodate to his style. Be on the lookout for several important categories of style. The chances are your professor's style will fall into one of them.

The Fact-Lover

Some professors love to shower their students with facts—the more the better. Their courses tend to be geared toward memorization with little time spent on creative thinking. You will need to understand whatever concepts are employed in stating the facts and also how to apply your knowledge, but your professor will likely emphasize knowing the facts. This sort of approach is much more common in introductory courses and, of course, in more fact-driven subjects like history than in applied ones like mathematics. But the subject matter alone doesn't dictate whether the emphasis is on facts; your professor is the one who decides what to teach and test.

Fact-lovers are pretty easy to detect. If your professor lectures solely by presenting information and spends little time on explanations, discussions, or problems, he's probably got a fact-fetish. Look also to his tests and quizzes: do the answers call for lists of identifications, the details of court cases, or descriptions of cellular processes? Success in these classes hinges on how much of the information you are able to cram and repeat.

Conversely your ability to discuss the subject intelligently and deeply might count for little in this class. If the professor simply does not care about your opinion or ability to apply the knowledge critically, prepare yourself to internalize lots of information. As distasteful as rote memorization may be, it may be your most efficient method. Focus on the flashcards and save time on the rest.

The Problem Solver

A radically different type of professor is the problem solver. In a problem solver's class the emphasis is on—you guessed it—solving problems. Of course, you will need facts to solve problems, but the key to success in her class is getting the right answer. Many math and science classes are conducted in this manner, but not all of them. Other disciplines also have professors who emphasize problem solving. As always there is no way to know her type before her class begins. Don't assume you have one type or another until the class has started!

The problem solver spends a fair amount of his class time working through examples and regularly assigning problem sets for homework. His classes are generally essay-free, but still a lot of critical thinking is needed. The best strategy for these classes is practice, practice, and more practice. Read carefully to learn strategies. Memorization might not be of much help here. Pay attention to the *kinds* of problems he focuses on. These are the ones you will need to understand and be able to solve. If your calculus teacher spends a lot of time on exact antiderivatives but glosses over approximation techniques, don't kill yourself learning Riemann sum approximations. If he doesn't care about approximations, focus on exact techniques, and of course vice versa. Be sensitive to the type of questions your professor asks. Math classes are most likely to be taught by problem solvers but there are no guarantees. A mathematician we know taught linear algebra one summer—a mid-level math class normally consisting of problems and not much else—and got "carried away." He wound up requiring his students to know every proof in the book and had no time for anything else. A perfect fact-lover, at least for that summer. But don't assume that because a teacher was a problem solver in one class that he'll be one in every class—teachers change styles to suit content, and it's up to you to be flexible.

The Critical Evaluator

A third basic type is the critical evaluator. Here we have in mind a professor who is very concerned with *your* thoughts about the material. Are you able to come up with your own view? Can you defend that view? This sort of professor typically devotes a lot of class time to discussion and expects everyone to participate. The material she presents often consists of opposing views with no obvious "correct" answers to the questions she raises.

Don't make the mistake of thinking that your opinions are *all* that matters for his classes, though. Attention to students' views doesn't mean truth and reason have taken a vacation. You need to ensure that you have understood the materials he has presented and know enough about them to support whatever view you want to push. Pay attention to understanding the various positions presented in lectures and readings, but don't fret over exact details like dates, for example. These classes usually require essays—either essay tests, take-home papers, or assignments. When essays are the testing format you have some leeway with what you need to know. You aren't expected to know only cold, hard facts. Of course, you'll need to know what you're talking about and be able to support your view. Make sure you know what you need to know to present a clear and convincing case for your position, but remember that in this case *understanding* the materials is a lot more important than memorizing them. Spend time also developing your own interpretation and preparing to argue for it.

It's important to detect the degree of freedom and level of creativity that a teacher expects and will permit in her classes. See if she cares most about your understanding the materials or about forming your own positions. Does she spend most of the time teaching solo with her discussion focused strictly on the lecture topic? Or does she go out of her way to elicit class opinions? Is she happy as long as the discussion is lively, even if off-topic? These signs should clue you in as to how you should spend your time. If she cares more about the material, work hard to understand it and be able to explain it in your essays. If she cares more about original thought, work hard on formulating your own unique viewpoint.

A Combination

Just as people rarely fit one personality type or another, your professor probably won't fit neatly into one of the above categories. She will likely exhibit characteristics of each. Your job is to pay attention to which ones are most salient. Chances are she will belong *mostly* to one type. But whatever her teaching style, think about what she wants from you. Keep in mind the wide differences in what's required from each kind. No single formula (such as "do every problem in the book") can help you get the most out of every class. It's really up to you to figure out what is needed to succeed.

This brings us around to an extremely important point. When it comes to being a good student there are no Ten Commandments. What a student must do in order to succeed in any classroom is not written in stone. You are in the domain of a single teacher. For the purposes of his course, he is the boss. So, try listening to him; try to determine as best you can what he expects from his students. And then try to do that—taking into account reasonableness and your other commitments.

Of course, you need to distinguish unreasonable from reasonable demands. If you see that your teacher has unreasonable expectations before the class begins or early enough for you to change classes, do so. If a teacher assigns a different book to read every week or a paper for every lecture, she's insensitive to your need to balance assignments in this course with assignments in others. Demanding teachers can teach you a lot, but not if their demands make it impossible for you to learn anything in any other course.

On Classroom Comportment

Even once you have come up with a clear idea of the professor's expectations, your work isn't over. You want your teacher to be actively interested in you. Failing to attract his interest in you as a student can make it harder for you to learn from him, and having him interested in you certainly can't hurt. If your teacher doesn't take you seriously and doesn't care about your progress, you're on your own. Worse fates can befall you, but wouldn't it be better to have your teacher as an ally?

Your chances of learning increase the more sympathetic your teacher is to you. You want her to perceive you as a student who is first and foremost intent on learning. Having a professor take an interest in your mind and be sincerely concerned that you have understood her fully can be a rich and rewarding experience.

Seating Arrangements

You have control over whether your teacher thinks you're really interested in her course. In every classroom someone has to sit in the back, but no one is obliged to make a habit of it. Students who regularly gravitate toward the rear do so for a variety of reasons. They might have courses scheduled across campus and always arrive late. They might be shy and believe that the back of the room protects them from having to answer questions or enter into class discussion. Unfortunately, this strategy is extremely effective. Teachers often take less notice of students who sit in the rear. Even if it's untrue, teachers tend to think that students who sit in the back are less interested in learning than those who sit in the front. Assuming this isn't true for you, go ahead and sit up front.

Students who sit up front are literally in the teacher's face. He asks them questions much more often than those in the back, which gives them more opportunities to score points. They get encouraged to be involved, and it's much harder for them to just zone out. Their assignments or responses get discussed, improved, or corrected in class. This sort of learning is invaluable. It's as if they were in a private tutorial, even though several hundred other students may be in the room. So make a habit of arriving early and working your way into vacancies toward the front early in the semester. Habits form quickly, and students are creatures of habit. After a while, your classmates won't dare take your place even when you arrive late. Everyone has staked out a place and habitually occupies it.

Of course, maybe you can't take a seat up front, especially if you're traveling all the way across campus or if you have another class immediately before. Tell the professor you have to arrive late and sit in the back of the room. Apologize beforehand for any disruptions. It's not the best possible scenario, but if you're forced to be tardy, let her know that you care enough to inform her and that it's beyond your control to change it. Do the same if you have to leave early, even if it doesn't affect where you sit. She'll appreciate the courtesy. Professors often get thrown when students come in late or leave early; knowing that it isn't because their class is too boring helps. These little conversations also help make you familiar to your professor. How much should you care that your professors know you? It's easy to believe in the benefits of anonymity. No one notices if you aren't in class; no one cares if you haven't done the assignment. Why would you want to have the professor recognize you at all? For one thing these alleged benefits aren't benefits at all; feeling pressured to keep up is not exactly a bad thing! There are many advantages to being known: opportunities, recommendations, contacts—all these follow from being recognized, as we'll point out many times in this book. One advantage is so near and dear to every student's heart that it's worth noting now: when it comes to grading, if you're familiar, you're more likely to get the benefit of the doubt.

Most students assume that grading is a fair and reliable process. Since they spend about four years being judged on their grades, it really should be. But it isn't. We aren't talking about all-out corruption, or even anything close, but about human factors that affect everyone. We want to see people we like succeed. Professors take longer with the exams and papers of the students they know, and they are more likely to give them the benefit of the doubt. These subjective aspects of grading—and there are many—will favor you if your teacher knows and likes you. There can be less of a difference between an A and a B or a B and a C than you might think. Sometimes the difference is arbitrary and having the professor know you can be all it takes. (We'll come back to this in detail in Chapter 4.)

Classroom Manners

Another reason not to sit in the back of the room is that the farther you are from your teacher the more likely you are to become bored and start reading the school newspaper or chatting with friends. You stand the risk of distracting your professor and making a bad impression. This seems obvious but each semester some group of students enjoys the crossword puzzle, takes naps, or otherwise ignores this point—at their peril.

Most professors adopt a policy that students are adults and should take responsibility for themselves. A teacher may say that he doesn't care whether his students attend every lecture, hand in every assignment, or attend any office hours. But don't take such casual comments at face value. Professors are people; they don't always mean what they say. When professors announce that all they care about is that their students learn the course materials and do well on the final exam or final paper or project, don't believe them for a moment. No one wants to lecture to an empty hall or to a wall of newspapers. Trust us on this one—would *you* want to?

Certain behaviors will *always* be construed as rude; sleeping, reading newspapers, yawning frequently, having private conversations, and other signs of boredom are guaranteed to annoy your professor big time. Conversely he'll automatically warm up to those who look like they're paying attention. Eye contact goes a long way here; it shows you are interested and attentive. As a rule of thumb, try to imagine you're talking one-on-one with the teacher and behave accordingly.

Just as making a good impression can open doors for you and protect your grade, making a bad impression can be a disaster. The last thing you want is for your professor to be annoyed with you while she is grading. If she thinks you are inattentive and bored in class, you've lost points before she's even picked up your paper. This isn't vindictiveness on her part. She probably won't even realize she's penalizing you. But professors automatically assume that students who don't *seem* to be paying attention aren't learning as much as those who do, so they're already inclined to be less charitable.

This negative assessment has consequences only if your professor knows your name; many students count on anonymity to protect them. As long as the professor has no idea who they are, they can suffer no consequences. True, but why would you want to commit to anonymity—never participating, never seeking help, never interacting at all? That's a high price for the freedom to do a crossword puzzle during class.

Even the most liberal teachers are easily insulted (even when no insult was intended) when students are indifferent or rude. You may not take yourself to be acting badly. You may be bored or sleepy and figure nothing much will happen if you indulge. You might think your professors are indifferent to whether you read the newspaper or not; if a teacher is concerned, you might think he'll say so out loud, just like your high school teachers would have. Don't make any such assumptions. College teachers will rarely humiliate a student in class—lectures might be more entertaining if they did—but silence shouldn't be taken as complaisance. Professors are aware at some level of most everything you do in their classrooms. Don't assume they aren't forming deep impressions about you. They are—whether consciously or not.

Participation

One of the best ways to make sure that your professor's deep impression of you is a positive one is to participate in class. Participating is a great way to get to know the professor and to become a student he knows and looks out for. That relationship is the starting point for so much else, as we'll see in later chapters, and has immediate benefits when it comes time to grade. There are so many reasons to participate; why are so many students reluctant to do so?

Some students are too embarrassed to raise their hands in class. Often they feel that their question will sound stupid or their answer will be wrong. They may not want to draw attention to themselves because they're shy and prefer anonymity. Other students are just too apathetic in class. They aren't interested in the discussion and can't be bothered joining in. Avoid anonymity and apathy. They won't get you anywhere. If you're reading this book, chances are you care about your classes, so apathy shouldn't be a big issue for you. Get involved!

It's harder for those who feel self-conscious or shy to participate. Anyone who feels this way suffers needlessly from low classroom self-esteem. If you're genuinely confused about something, there's a huge chance others are too. If you answer incorrectly, others would have also gotten it wrong. You might worry that the people who aren't confused or who would have gotten it right will think less of you for asking or being wrong. Don't! As long as you don't go overboard and end up questioning every statement the professor makes, she has no right or reason to think twice about it. And remember: *you* were the one brave enough to volunteer.

Asking Questions

Even if your self-esteem is low, within reason you're better off adopting a bold stance; if you're confused, many others must be. If you don't know a solution to a problem, then treat it as an important issue that must be solved. Should you have a question that no one else is asking, assume that this is because no one else has enough self-confidence to ask it. See yourself as a hero performing an invaluable service for the rest of the class simply by raising your hand. As a lark you might represent yourself as speaking on behalf of the entire class, addressing the teacher as their ambassador.

It's especially important to feel confident enough to ask questions. If you don't, you may remain confused. You deserve to be clear about the materials. Don't get left behind or in the dark. Like everything else, asking questions should be done in moderation. You should engage your teacher without alienating him (or the entire rest of the class). A compulsive questioner wastes everyone's time including her own. Sometimes the teacher will tell you to shut up; sometimes the moans and groans of your classmates will indicate that you've gone too far. Hogging airtime to an extreme makes everyone tired of you. With that in mind, it's still better to ask too many questions than to be silent. Just remember to be sensitive and to listen to yourself. If you're always the only one talking or if you're significantly slowing down the class, ease up. Learn to distinguish the big from the small, and to limit yourself to the most important questions.

Staying Relevant

Successful participation doesn't mean blurting out any question that pops into your head. Put effort and some preparation into what you say in class. Ask yourself whether your question or comment is relevant to what the professor is currently discussing. Is it at least on topic? The question may well need to be answered, but irrelevant questions can slow the class down and annoy people. However, being considerate of others doesn't mean you should forget about your questions. If you have an important question that isn't relevant to the current discussion, ask it after class. As always, what the masses think is important and what is important to you aren't always the same.

The majority of questions asked *during* class should be ones that most of the class can understand and appreciate. They should be relevant to mastering the material. You might have more advanced questions—ones that extend the material or delve deeper into it—or you might disagree with something presented. These questions are appropriate once in a while but if you consistently want to ask them, do so after class or in office hours. The rest of the class will probably not benefit much from your exchanges, so it's unfair to regularly take up their lecture time. These questions are extremely important, though, and absolutely should be asked—the only difference is when.

Professors don't like to give repeat performances. So if you intend to ask your professor a question, particularly in class, make sure it's not one he already answered. Especially avoid asking questions you'd know the answer to if only you hadn't missed class the other day. Few things are more likely to make a teacher feel he's wasting his time than having to repeat the same material over and over again.

Jot down your questions as they come to you. This technique helps you phrase them more clearly. If they're not appropriate to ask at that time, you won't forget them later. If you're unsure about their relevance, see how they look when written. If they're clear and pertinent, put in your two cents.

One of the most important times for asking questions is during review sessions before exams. Many professors hold these sessions as a way to let students clarify any issues they have with the material. If your class is having one, we strongly urge you to study *before* you attend it. Review sessions help much more if you've studied in advance, since questions normally crop up while studying. You can prepare questions to ask as you're studying, and make sure they get answered at the review session. Realizing the night before the exam that you've got a pressing question won't do you any good at all. Come prepared to find out what you need to know.

Not all questions are good questions, though. Stay away from questions of the sort: "Do we have to know this for the exam?" Though all too frequently asked, it's guaranteed to annoy your professor. The topic might have been covered only briefly in class, or might not fit in with the rest of the course, so you may want to know whether to study it at all. Still, asking the question is not the way to find out. Questions about the format, content, and length of the exam will bore your professor and won't help you learn. They will only waste review time.

Fortunately, you have other ways to uncover a topic's importance. The perfect strategy is to bring that topic up during the review session (or during office hours if no such session occurs). If the professor has no intention of testing you on a subject, he will probably not waste his or your time reviewing it. If he doesn't devote any time to the topic, it will pretty definitely not make it to the exam; and if he does, then you'll end up with a better grasp of it anyway. You have the information you need (more, if he actually goes over the topic), and, to boot, you haven't alienated your professor.

Answering Questions

Answering questions works a lot like asking them. When called upon to answer a question, either say you don't know the answer or answer assertively. You receive no kudos for hesitation. Even if you're right, the teacher will figure that you guessed. Answering confidently won't make you seem overbearing; exuding confidence isn't the same as having an attitude. But answering hesitantly suggests you're uncertain. Assuming you have at least some grasp of the material, trust yourself. Odds are you'll be *at least* partly right.

Many teachers look for voluntary participants. Here you can gain so much by taking part. Professors are often grateful to have someone offering to answer questions. It shows that the class is not (entirely) asleep. You'll find that professors return to the same group of students repeatedly, and ultimately that group receives special consideration. By volunteering you'll appear confident and interested, and the teacher will become aware of who you are. You'll get to be a member of the inner sanctum. Enjoy the benefits!

Being a Savvy Consumer

Teachers can be unclear; they can even be as unclear as their students. Sometimes they're unprepared; sometimes they're incapable of explaining the material appropriately. Every teacher has lapses and bad moments, some a lot more than others. In the latter cases the problem isn't lack of clarity; it's more lack of teaching ability.

Here's a little tidbit that you might not have known: although grammar school and high school teachers are obliged by state law to have taken courses in pedagogy, university professors aren't. Your teacher may have had no training in teaching whatever. Your class might even be the first time he has ever taught the subject, or worse: the first time he has ever taught at all. From this perspective it's amazing that so many university professors can teach as well as they do.

What should you do when your professor is unclear to you? Don't necessarily assume your professor is to blame. It could be you. If you don't understand her, either you're unprepared or she isn't making herself clear. If it's the latter, do what you can to get her to clarify and explain. Asking questions is the best strategy, particularly if you sense widespread agreement among your classmates about her problem. Don't be obnoxious. But don't forget that you are in effect employing this person to teach you. You are the consumer. When your teacher is not doing her job effectively, you have a right to courteously request clarity. If you ordered a steak in a restaurant and got a piece of bread instead, you would complain. You wouldn't figure that,

well, these things happen and at least you are getting something to eat, so you shouldn't protest. Why should it be any different for an enterprise significantly more important, expen-
sive, and time-consuming? Given the sacrifices that attending
college exacts from you and your family, you have a right to expect a quality education. Your questions need be no cleverer
than saying that you didn't understand what your professor
had just said. Could she amplify or clarify, please.

Conclusion

Classroom comportment is extremely important but can also
be extremely tricky. There is no guaranteed formula for successful behavior in all circumstances. The most constant and important points to remember are as follows:

✔ Be sensitive to the professor's expectations and be willing
to adjust to them.

✔ Sit in the front of the classroom and show you're listening.

✔ Ask and answer questions confidently and willingly.

✔ Remember you have a right to expect the lecture to be clear
and comprehensive.

Bearing in mind the last suggestion, how do you balance your
desire to learn with a desire to avoid alienating your professor?
Listen to yourself. As long as you are polite and your questions
are taken seriously, you're doing fine. As we have indicated
many times throughout, your teacher is only human. He has a
tolerance level, which may or may not be reasonable. He has
his likes and dislikes, which may or may not be appropriate. He
may or may not be flexible. He may or may not care about your
education. He may think that teaching is only one small part
of his job and that his research is much more important. You

have no control over his motives, desires, or ambitions. But whatever they are, what's ultimately important is how well he teaches. If he is a good teacher, you win. If not, you have your work cut out for you. Circumstances are not always this clear-cut, though.

Two equally bright students may sit through the very same set of lectures with equal devotion, yet one thinks the teacher is terrific and the other thinks her incompetent. Teaching evaluations often show as much disagreement as movie reviews. Though the two students are intellectual equals, their personalities and expectations may differ. Virtually everyone dislikes somebody. Your teacher's personality may clash with yours. But the more distance you put between yourself and your teacher the less likely you are to learn anything from her. Avoid those encounters that are likely to accentuate your differences. Do your best to learn what you need to under the circumstances.

We're only asking you to use common sense. Although you may be able to talk with your teacher about your differences, you can't count on it. Both your authors have had teachers with whom we didn't get along. In retrospect we might have done better to have dropped those classes. In a few cases we did. Don't get paranoid, though. Not every difference in personality necessarily leads to a poor learning experience. You know who you are. If you can figure out who your teacher is, you can try to adjust to him (within reason) for the term—particularly if you are interested in the material. You don't have to marry him; you want what's in his head, not his heart. Ask yourself how you intend to survive his class. Should you avoid asking questions or attending office hours? If your strategies require more than you think you can swallow, drop the course. Not every class is wonderful; sometimes you just run into bad luck. But you'll have winners too, especially if you follow the advice in the previous chapter. Find as many of them as you can; getting an education is hard enough without having to do pop psychology on your professor.

CASE STUDIES

William's Problem

After completing his core requirements (read: after an eternity), William decided he should begin more advanced classes. He has enrolled in two difficult classes—one political science and one history—and wants to do everything he can to do well in them. He's always thought that history requires a lot of memorization; certainly it was this way in high school. He had never really encountered political science before but always vaguely imagined the field was based on heated discussions. The classes have been under way for a few weeks—long enough for the add-drop date to pass—but they aren't turning out as he would have predicted. The political science professor rarely gives the students a chance to discuss the material, and the lectures are mostly geared toward understanding the details and chronology of various court cases. The teacher gives out many reading assignments; most focus on facts, a few address larger political issues. The course is not nearly as discussion-oriented as William had hoped.

The history lecturer is a different story. He doesn't hold discussions, but his lectures are not simple presentations of facts. Often he elaborates on the causes and implications of whatever they're studying; he also gave his first quiz recently. William had studied hard for it and knew the material inside out. The quiz consisted of a single essay, requiring the students to put the current topic (the Spanish American War) in the context of America's economic situation at the time—*not* a simple regurgitation of facts. William did fairly well on it but wondered if he might have saved some time studying, as he had memorized every single date and place associated with the war.

The Solution

William needs to be more sensitive to his professors' expectations. William is managing to keep his grades up, but he could do much better if he modified his study habits. His preconceived notions of the subject matter were mistaken. Although he is disappointed, his disappointment is beside the point. The political science professor may not be teaching the class as William expected or wanted, but William is enrolled and essentially at his teacher's mercy. The lectures are focused on long lists of facts—a good indication that profound essays are not going to be called for. As the professor is concerned mostly with information, his exams will probably focus on that aspect. William is of course free to read more conceptual papers on his own, but for the exam he should pay careful attention to the details.

The first history quiz is a good sign that the professor is less concerned with lists of facts than with overall thought and understanding. His lecture style is harder to categorize. Although he focuses on the conceptual, he doesn't encourage class discussion. Understandably, William wasn't sure quite what to expect on the quiz, but now he knows that he should expect something similar on the exams. While knowing precise dates is certainly not a bad thing, William should not focus on such details at the expense of the concepts. As a study exercise for this class, William should work on being able to place the events they discuss into the larger context of the times. He needs to spend time understanding how different events and historical forces have influenced each other.

As time will not permit William to learn *everything*, he ought to think carefully about the aspects important to each class. There is no straight formula for an ideal study pattern, or for an ideal student. It's all a matter of flexibility. With this in mind, William needs to revise his study attitude for both classes, making sure that he knows all the details for his political science class and that he keeps his eye on the big picture for the history class.

Lucy's Problem

Lucy is a bright, hard-working sophomore with a GPA of 3.5 out of a possible 4.0. While she is happy with her grades, she often feels that her professors haven't a clue as to who she is. She is not particularly outgoing—socially she prefers to stick to a group of close friends rather than making casual acquaintances. Her pleasant yet introverted nature is reflected in her classroom behavior. Although she is never talkative or demanding and always pays attention, she feels self-conscious and is generally passive in class. As a result many of her professors never even learn her name.

If Lucy doesn't know how to solve a problem in physics class, she relies on her textbook to learn how to do it. If the book is no help (as is too often the case), she is relieved if someone else in class asks for her. Fortunately, her grades haven't suffered yet, and she figures she understands enough to do well. Sometimes she worries about taking advanced courses and wishes she had the confidence to speak up when she is confused.

The most frustrating part of class for Lucy, though, happens when she does understand the material. The professors will often ask questions she knows the answers to, but she doesn't let on. More outgoing students shoot their hands up right away. The professors always know their names and clearly think highly of them. When no one answers, Lucy is incredibly frustrated. The professors always seem annoyed that apparently no one is paying attention. She is, but they don't know it.

The Solution

The best way for Lucy to overcome her shyness is to practice gradually. She would be best to start with situations where she is confident of the answer to the question, particularly if no one else is trying to answer it. Even if she gets the answer wrong, she can take pride in being the only one brave enough to try. Moving her seat up to the front row would encourage her to participate. Attending an office hour can also help build the sort of relationship between her and her teacher that will make voicing her opinion in class more comfortable for her. It's easier to tell someone you know what's on your mind. Even a single visit to an office hour can make classroom exchanges not only less stressful but fun. Nothing can boost self-confidence more than knowing your teacher is on your side.

Once Lucy becomes more practiced at answering questions, she should try asking questions herself. Attempting to figure the problem out on her own is still a good strategy, but if she doesn't succeed, she needs to ask for help. Through her voluntary participation, her professors will come to know her better and she'll feel more relaxed in class, so it will be easier for her to speak up when she has questions. Her professors' attention to her will make it more difficult for her to hide her confusion. Ultimately, she'll gain a lot of confidence and do better in her classes.

---

3 Outside the Classroom
Cultivating Relationships with Good Teachers

Even the most outgoing students can expect only limited contact with their professors while in the classroom. No teacher—good or bad—can (or should) focus on a single student for an extended period of class time. But outside the classroom these opportunities abound. Students can clear up confusions, have their questions answered fully, and go much deeper into the material, even pursuing independent research. Contact outside the classroom also lays the foundation for developing a professional relationship.

Contact is hard to overestimate. Although most professors try to make sure their lectures are understandable, any given presentation might fly right over a student's head. Sometimes other students can help, but relying on them isn't always a good idea. There's a tacit guarantee that the professor knows the material. Assuming that other students know what they are talking about could be a big mistake. In a one-on-one situation a good teacher should be able to explain the material much better than a student could. An office hour is a quick remedy for many a muddle. Clearing up confusion can make you feel more relaxed and confident about the course. The professor will often end up going beyond the required material, giving you new insights and a privileged status.

According to a common myth, office hours are only for students in trouble; students who understand the material fully don't need them. Wrong! Discussing the subject with a professor can bring a subject matter to life in a way that an everyday lecture can't. Your first meeting with your professor can even lead to a special project, another great way to interact and develop a relationship.

Of course, merely showing up to office hours is not enough. Getting the most out of your visit always takes some care and preparation, but the benefits of academic support and reliable contacts are well worth the effort.

Approaching the Teacher

In many schools, professors are required to hold regular office hours. Even if your professor has a set time to be in her office, make an appointment. Most professors are busy. Sometimes they miss their office hours. Scheduling an appointment in advance is more than polite; it could save you a lost afternoon.

Arrange the appointment in person after class. Keeping track of student appointments might not rank top among your teacher's priorities, though, so make the process as painless for her as possible. Ask if she would like you to e-mail her. She can easily put an e-mail appointment in her diary; it's harder for her to do that in an emptying classroom. If this is your first private contact with your professor, this meeting affords you the chance to introduce yourself. The more familiar you are to your professor the more concern and attention you will receive.

It's not always easy to approach your professor. Some students have no trouble doing so; they are wholly relaxed and confident with their instructors. Others aren't so lucky. You may feel shy and awkward approaching the teacher. Maybe she doesn't seem like the warmest person, or maybe you feel self-conscious approaching her. Remember, though, that you have every right to make an appointment to see her. This first encounter needn't be long at all; just introduce yourself, and say you'd like to set up a time to meet with her. Will she be in office hours this week? Give her a specific time and confirm that she can make it. Thank her, and say you'll see her then. Easy!

One obvious point is that you should know your professor's name. (Professors are continually amazed when students cannot recall the name of a teacher they had just the term before or, even worse, someone they are taking that very term!) You also want her to know *your* name, which is another reason to also e-mail her. Sending an e-mail provides her with one more reminder should your poor, absent-minded professor forget who you are. And believe us—it happens.

Whenever e-mailing a professor, less is more! Keep your message as brief as possible. A lot of professors will only skim long e-mails anyway. Be sure to send an e-mail that will show your current return e-mail address. Perhaps give your telephone number, so your professor can reach you if she needs to reschedule. In your e-mail, if you're asking a question, make the question prominent and don't include anything that isn't necessary. The more extraneous material the more likely your main point will be overlooked.

Office Hours Comportment

Once you've made your appointment, you have two main concerns: how to conduct yourself and how to ask questions. The questions you ask have a huge impact on the results you get, as we'll discuss in the next section, "Asking for Help." That concern aside, to form a strong relationship or in some cases just to get your questions answered, you need to pay attention to how you act.

A Routine Visit

Our first point should go without saying: Don't be late! Promptness is important in every professional situation and office hour visits are no exception. Being late is a sign of disrespect; it indicates that you think your professor's time is less valuable than your own. Remember who assigns your grade! If you show up late, don't be surprised if your professor is annoyed, especially if you're casual about being tardy.

We don't have any sneaky tricks for making the professor eat out of your hand. (Bribery has a grand history, but not in academia.) Remember, teachers are human. Courtesy, pleasantness, and general good manners are as appealing to them as they are to other people. Kissing up is also a time-honored strategy, but most professors see through brown-nosers. Gushing over what a beautiful tie your professor is wearing is only going to embarrass you both. However, if you happen to see a portrait of your favorite author on his wall, a comment on that is appropriate. The difference is that one situation is contrived, the other natural. You don't need to fawn. Be relaxed and respectful. Common courtesy, of course, entails greeting the professor upon arriving and thanking him upon leaving.

People tend to relax around relaxed people. Some people are better at putting people at their ease than others. Some professors will automatically begin with friendly, open attitudes. But don't be surprised or flustered if your professor doesn't. If your professor is easygoing, you don't need to be tense or shy with him. If he's formal or dismissive, don't allow yourself to be intimidated. Don't infer that just because he seems uncomfortable that he doesn't like you; more often than not he's just an uncomfortable kind of guy, no matter whom he's with. As long as you're polite and not demanding or unpleasant, it's most unlikely that he'll have a problem with you, so don't sweat it. If he isn't an outgoing person, your being tense is only going to make him more uncomfortable. Be warm and pleasant and then watch him relax!

Interacting with professors is no different from interacting with anyone else. As a rule of thumb, behave with professors as you do with peers that you don't know very well. Be polite, pleasant, and friendly. The vast majority of professors respond well to students who treat them as people rather than as authority figures.

That said, remember you're not actually in an equal relationship with your professor. He is the boss. Pay attention to the kind of person he is. Some people welcome familiarity more than others. Be sensitive to cues that give you permission: does he lean back comfortably in his chair or sit perched at the edge? Does he engage you in casual conversation? No matter his signals, though, don't expect to be best buddies. Even with the most relaxed and informal teachers, don't forget who has the authority. The idea is to be pleasant and friendly but always respectful.

Don't expect your professor to do all the talking. Be prepared academically (as we will discuss in the next section). Try also to be clear, focused, and to keep the discussion flowing. Being prepared and ready with an agenda doesn't mean that you should be arrogant or demanding. It means you need to clarify your reasons for visiting. Begin your discussion by stating your reasons for requesting a meeting. You also need to have the confidence to lay down the issues that brought you to her office, so that you can both stay on task. When your professor talks, listen. Zoning out is guaranteed to annoy her a lot. She didn't request the meeting; you did. Imagine being asked to hang out with someone who then yawns in your face all night! Remember, because she's human, don't expect her to be more understanding than anyone else. Be grateful if she is.

Worst Case Scenario

An office hour may launch a working relationship, but you would be presumptuous to expect an office visit to result in serious bonding. You do, however, have a right to get the help you need. In Chapter 1 we discussed criteria for choosing an instructor; one was accessibility. Not every teacher is eager and willing to help, and you can easily end up with a dismissive one. If you detect that your instructor has no interest in his students, you may not want to visit him at all, which is quite understandable.

But what if a visit is necessary? Suppose you're having trouble in a class with an inaccessible professor. You have several options. If you know another professor in the field, consider asking her for help. Sometimes fellow students can help out also, but bear in mind that students aren't experts and can misinform you despite their good intentions.

If none of these options is open, however, you have little choice, so go ahead and approach your own professor. Prepare your questions carefully. (See the following section.) If your inquiries are vague or ill conceived, your professor will have an easier time dismissing you. But even if you plan your questions carefully, your professor may be unresponsive or unhelpful. Some instructors—shocking though it may seem—will cut students off straightaway, telling them to figure it out for themselves or to try again. If you've genuinely made every effort to understand the material yourself, you may need to be more assertive (in a polite way). Let him know you aren't visiting him out of laziness but out of a real need for help. Few teachers will refuse to help in the face of a mature, earnest and courteous request. Quite honestly, if your teacher does refuse, he probably has bigger problems than just being an inadequate teacher. But be sincere, as professors see through students who profess to be trying but really aren't.

Don't get discouraged whatever happens. If the instructor turns out to be atrocious, focus on doing well in his class despite or even to spite him! Besides, the majority of your professors—providing you've taken care in choosing them—will be helpful. Office hours are usually fruitful; our goal is to help you make them as fruitful as possible.

Asking for Help

Asking the right questions is important. Few valuable meetings ever begin with the student saying, "I'm confused. Could you go over all the stuff again?" Asking a professor to cover materials from a wide range of lectures is almost always inappropriate. (An extended but excused absence is an exception.) If you've attended every lecture but are still confused, you have little reason to think that a trip to an office hour is going to help. If the material was incomprehensible when spread out over three months, why would it be more accessible when squeezed into an hour? The more general the question the less you'll benefit. Your professor might not even know where to begin. Showing up with a blanket complaint is like hiring people to work on your house without saying what it is you want them to do. When the workers ask what jobs you want done, you tell them you just want them to generally improve the house. Unless you're specific with your requests, it's hard to ever get the results you're looking for. For one, if you yourself don't know what your problem is, how do you expect someone else to figure it out?

The Scope of the Problem

The more focused and specific your question the better. The professor is not going to reteach the entire course; if he did, it would be so rushed that you wouldn't benefit much anyway. Perhaps there's a certain topic you didn't understand. Pinpoint exactly which aspect of that topic is giving you the most trouble. If you aren't specific, your professor may just repeat what he said in class and your initial confusion will remain. So invest some time in preparing questions. The better they are, the better the answers will be. You may want to write them up beforehand, which will help you organize your thoughts. If you're struggling with a specific problem or passage, bring examples along. In short, be prepared.

Some courses will leave you with more than just a specific question, but few professors are happy to become tutors for their students. It's not their job. If clearing up your confusion will take up an inordinate amount of your teacher's time—say, more one-on-one visits than there are office hours, then short of moving in with him, get yourself a student tutor. (Sometimes tutoring is available free of charge. See if your school has a learning resource center.) If you have questions the tutor can't answer, then bring *those* to the professor's attention.

Always try first to understand the material yourself. If nothing else, your effort should help you shape more direct questions. Sometimes students feel lost and unable to describe what it is they don't understand. Avoid going to office hours in this state of confusion. Unless your teacher is extremely patient and not very busy, your blank stare when he asks what you don't understand won't elicit from him the sort of help you need. Try studying the book or enlisting the help of a classmate until you can pinpoint the problem.

Missed Lectures

Don't pepper an office hour with questions about missed lectures. If you know beforehand that you have to miss a class, arrange (with the professor's permission) to have that lecture taped. Failing this, find a competent note-taker and ask her if you can photocopy her notes. However, note taking is an enterprise usually reserved for private consumption. It is typically abbreviated, sometimes with private codes. More often borrowing notes is a counterproductive strategy. But if you do borrow notes, and if you don't understand something in those notes, ask the professor if he can elaborate on what he meant, but keep these questions to a minimum, as often such exchanges can be frustrating for both the teacher and the student. It's too easy to get the Prufrock response: "I never meant that at all" or "I never said that."

If your problem stems from missed lectures, you have no reason to expect the professor to take extra time to reteach the lost materials for you. You shouldn't have missed in the first place. Don't skip classes! If it's too late for that advice to matter, you have your work cut out for you. Study the reading material as best you can and find a fellow student (or even better, two of them) willing to help. Only after you actually have a notion of what's going on should you initiate a meeting with the professor. Ultimately attending class is easier and a good deal less work. Trust us on this one.

Timing

Let's assume that you've been attending class regularly and keeping up with assignments, so your confusion isn't a result of negligence. Here's the golden rule: *Ask for clarification as soon as a problem arises.* Don't wait until the course has moved on to another topic. Most courses are cumulative; usually problems don't clear up as the course goes on. Rather they're likely to get worse until they're beyond salvaging. Continuing blindly until the final weeks is going to leave you with an insoluble problem. Even if your initial confusion is finally straightened out, you may be left having to relearn the entire rest of the material within a few days. If, however, you voice your concerns as soon as they crop up, your problem won't multiply throughout the rest of the course. Asking your professor to help with a focused problem is appropriate; asking him to reteach the course in light of it is not.

If your question is manageable and can be cleared up in a reasonable amount of time, still be aware of *when* you ask it. Avoid the impression that your only concern is the final grade. Visiting the professor on the day of an exam—or a day or two before—often (to be honest, invariably) leaves exactly this impression. Other students are also coming in at the end of the semester, and you may not receive the attention you need. So even in a noncumulative class, clear up problems as soon as they arise. It's hard to imagine any good reason to procrastinate.

Appropriate Questions

Getting the most out of office hours is a complicated business. You might not always be sure about which questions are appropriate to ask, so try reviewing this checklist before you jump in there:

✔ Do I have a real question and not just a general complaint?

✔ Am I confused because I missed class?

✔ How quickly do I think my question can be answered?

✔ Can I learn anything more on my own to make my question narrower or more focused?

If you can tell that the question is too complicated or broad or that you have too many questions for the professor to answer in the allotted time, look into peer tutoring or try again to figure out the material yourself. Failing that, go ahead and ask but try not to get yourself into that situation. The surest way to keep your questions sharp and answerable is to ask them as early as you possibly can, although timeliness does not always result in sharpness.

Above and Beyond

The preceding section dealt with requesting help, but getting help isn't the only good reason to attend office hours. Meeting one-on-one with a professor offers a unique and valuable opportunity to learn more about the subject. Although a few professors don't want to go beyond the class content, most professors worth their salt—as long as they aren't overwhelmed—are eager to engage enthusiastic students. Believe it or not, *you* might even be a valuable asset to *them* by, say, becoming involved in their research, so it's to their advantage to pay you some attention.

Sometimes the course material just captures your imagination and attention, prompting you to learn more. Office visits are the ideal way to pursue further involvement in the subject. Once again, don't come in with vague ideas. Invest some time and thought beforehand: Is there a special area you would like to know more about? Do you have an idea about a different approach to something mentioned in class? Would you like to know more about the professor's area of expertise or get some suggestions for extra reading material? Without having put any thought into your visit, you'll come off looking dull and uninteresting—or worse, stupid. But with a little preparation, you might wind up beginning a rewarding, perhaps even inspirational, relationship.

Departmental Talks

Many academic departments offer faculty and guest lectures. These activities provide a different perspective and more insight into the field. (But most importantly they frequently offer free food, sometimes even a soda.) If you're interested in learning more about the topic, attending these lectures is a great way to go about it. Most follow a similar format: an expert speaks for about an hour, then there is time at the end for questions. The talks aren't geared toward students, so you may not understand everything that's said. (If you don't understand something, avoid asking about it in the question-and-answer session. Those sessions are mostly to allow faculty in the audience to pick the speaker apart—which can be highly entertaining.)

If you happen to meet your professor at such an event, you have a great starting point for conversation. You might ask her what she thought about the presentation. You might even address her with a question on the material presented. Attendance at these talks underscores your interest in the field and can define you as a committed student. It also gives you the opportunity to see what's going on at the forefront of the field.

Special Projects

Some colleges require students to write a thesis in their senior year. These theses usually entail working closely with a faculty member, possibly doing individual research. Even if your college doesn't require a thesis, we recommend doing an independent project with a professor.

The Value of Independent Study

Don't think of independent studies simply as *more* class work. That's like thinking of playing professional basketball as just taking more gym classes. With few exceptions the general formats of classes are the same. The teacher relates other people's work to the students; the students absorb the material and demonstrate their recollection and understanding through exams and papers. The abilities necessary for success can include applying problem-solving techniques, regurgitating facts, or grasping the concepts presented. Opportunities for creative thought may seem to be limited, suggesting that academic success has little to do with creativity. But nothing could be further from the truth. Academic research is an extremely creative process, sometimes resulting in completely *new* knowledge.

Independent projects let students participate in research. You'll not only be absorbing facts, as is all too often the case in the classroom, but you'll also be encouraged to think for yourself. The professor will, needless to say, guide and assist you. No one expects you to come up with groundbreaking advances overnight. But research activity will develop your abilities in ways that a classroom education can't, and it can result in a different kind of learning taking place.

Selecting the Right Subject Matter

A long-term project is not something you should leap into blindly. As a rule of thumb, wait until your junior year to take one on. Of course, if the time is right before then, there's no obvious reason to wait. You can also begin a research project in your senior year as long as the idea has already been thought out. You'll have a problem accomplishing everything if you start entirely from scratch as a senior.

The first step is to decide which field you want to research. In most cases your major is the best choice, but other choices are possible. Consider the quality of your department; a department with only two faculty members probably won't provide the best opportunities. (Of course, this depends on the student-faculty ratio.) Consider your professional plans. If you're pre-med and majoring, for example, in Spanish with a minor in biology, you might be better off getting involved in a biology lab than writing a Spanish thesis. The experience in the laboratory is more closely related to your professional goals.

The most important consideration, though, is your level of excitement with the field. Special projects can involve a serious time commitment, so choosing one you have no interest in is a bad idea. You'll likely be uninspired and end up benefiting less. In most cases, a student's major and future plans don't conflict. If the idea of devoting any more time to your major is unappealing, shop around for a new one.

Selecting an Advisor

Once you have selected an area of interest, find an advisor and a specific project. The order may vary. You should have some idea of the topic that interests you within the field. For example, within psychology you may be interested in drug research rather than cognitive development. Once you have an idea of the topic, find faculty members interested in that topic. Visit faculty web pages or the department home page. They will often give information that will clue you in to a professor's areas of interest. Maybe you have taken a class that focused on the topic and know a suitable professor as a result.

If the professors who interest you run their own laboratories, your life is a bit easier. Most professors are all too eager to have students work cheaply or for free in their labs. Look on such servitude as good exploitation—everyone benefits. In this case you might not actually be pursuing a project of your own design but helping in the day-to-day workings of the lab. If you enjoy the work, your professor may be willing to give you more responsibility and you could end up (at least partly) running a project—possibly even getting paid!

If you're involved in a less technical discipline, setting up special projects is a little more difficult. The most standard form for special projects in such cases is the thesis (or an independent study course—see below). Here you'll need to have a more specific idea already planned. Your best bet is to find a professor whose class you have taken; perhaps something covered there sparked your interest. If so, that's an excellent starting point. Don't choose a teacher just because you received a good grade in her class. You'll need some genuine interest to make the project successful.

It's good practice to have some contact with the teacher before committing yourself to working with him. He may be too busy to guide you properly, or he may not be interested in working with students. You deserve to have guidance and interaction with your advisor and you should be able to rely on him. If he won't give this much, find someone else.

Laying the Foundation

Avoid having your proposal come out of the blue. You should have already established a working relationship with your professor. The most natural way is to take his class, but attending class isn't enough. A hundred or more other students may be enrolled, and he may not know you from Adam. The first step toward increasing your visibility is class participation. Most professors find that a small group of students—usually those in the front row—are the ones they interact with and come to know. Throughout this book we'll advise you to make yourself part of that group. It's probably the single best move you can make for your college career.

Interacting in class isn't enough to lay the foundation for independent study, though. We've emphasized the importance of out-of-class meetings throughout this chapter. Discussing the subject with your professor is the ideal way to lead into a special project. Ideally you could arrange such discussions for all your classes. Don't limit yourself to teachers you view as potential advisors. Before you entered college, you were only exposed to a limited number of subjects. At that stage few people know exactly what they want—and actually stick to it. Through your college experience you'll be introduced to new subjects, and you may find yourself interested in topics you previously ignored, overlooked, or disliked. You might plan to do a project in physics only to find yourself inspired by a linguistics professor. These discoveries are among the most valuable aspects of college life. Sometimes ideas for special projects just happen, especially in the course of discussion. You owe it to yourself to be open to these opportunities.

Formulating a Proposal

Entering a professor's lab is not difficult. Proposing a thesis is trickier. Although it's up to you to select a topic, expect your professor to give you input before settling on a final proposal. Sometimes ideas arise naturally in discussion. If not, the best strategy is to think of a question you'd like to see answered. Make the question broad rather than narrow. Then allow your advisor to guide you toward a more focused idea. This approach is better than beginning with a specific question that happens, unbeknownst to you, to be too difficult or impractical to address. Of course, this doesn't mean there's no such thing as too broad; your question should have some degree of focus. Certainly, after meeting with your advisor and deciding on a final idea, that idea should be very specific.

Your advisor won't want to hold your hand all the way through the project. Special projects are meant to be exercises in independent thinking. You will have to take some initiative. Rely on your advisor for support but don't expect her to do the work for you. You're wasting her time and yours if you just announce that you want to do something but have no idea what. One of the key differences between independent study and classroom work is that with the former the teacher won't always assign you a task. You are by and large responsible for most of the thinking yourself—and that's an important part of what makes these projects so valuable.

Following Through

Once you have established a proposal with an advisor, you need to get to work on it. Remember that you are going to do the bulk of the work. But don't let your advisor fade into the background on that account. Meet regularly to discuss your progress. These meetings will encourage you to stay on top of your work. Since your project will probably be a priority for you but not for your professor, you shouldn't expect her continual assistance and attention. Hounding and harrying your professor will only annoy her and make for a bad relationship. Still, she has agreed to advise you, and she ought to keep her end of the bargain and not abandon you.

Conclusion

Opportunities abound for learning outside of class. Working relationships with your professors can greatly enhance your academic experience and can be easily cultivated outside the lecture hall. Whether your interest is in understanding the material better or going beyond the classroom material, the strategies discussed here will help you make the most of your visits and any independent projects:

- ✔ Make yourself known: set up an appointment in person and then confirm via e-mail.
- ✔ Remember that your professor is human and deserving of courtesy and patience.
- ✔ Put in some thought beforehand: good questions receive good answers.
- ✔ Make an appointment as early as possible; never wait to the last minute.

✔ Use office hours to expand beyond topics discussed in class.

✔ Choose an area that interests you and do independent work in it.

As your relationship with your professor develops, your meetings may become more informal. Sometimes you'll be able just to kick back and relax. These visits can be fun! As for special projects, you might even find yourself writing a book!

CASE STUDIES

Mike's Problem

Mike is a biology major and generally does well enough in his classes. Although he sometimes leaves his assignments to the last minute, he usually gets away with procrastination. He hated math in high school, but now he needs to take Calculus I for his major. He really resents having to take the course. In the beginning the class didn't seem too difficult, just boring. He didn't pay much attention, and *somehow* the crossword puzzle often ended up on his desk during class. The first quiz results showed that he didn't have a handle on the material. Still, the quizzes didn't count for much, and the first major exam was several weeks off. So Mike decided to delay seeking help.

When the exam rolled around, Mike realized that the whole thing on derivatives had, well, passed him by. But he thought he could get his grade back up with the final exam, if only he learned the new material on integrals really well. He allowed himself the hope that integrals had little to do with derivatives, anyway. Within a week he realized that integrals had a lot to do with derivatives. Oops!

With only a short time left before the final, Mike sought his professor's help. He really couldn't afford to fail the class, and he knew he would if he didn't act right away.

The Solution

Mike's predicament could have been avoided, but that recognition gives him little comfort now. Nevertheless, he has a little time before his final exam, so he has some reason to hope. The first step for him is to pick up the book to see how much he gets from it. Math books are usually not designed for self-teaching, so this avenue may have limited benefit. Mike could get himself a tutor, invest in an online course designed for self-teaching, but he can expect to lose a lot of sleep. He may be able to separate the material, though, into what he can and can't follow. Then he might try to find a student tutor who can help him; she might be able at least to help him see which parts he doesn't understand. Once Mike has more of a handle on the material, the professor might be able to take him further to a more complete understanding. Much of the work is up to him now, though: locating the problem, and then working through it. The professor cannot possibly be expected to do it all for him at this stage.

Brian's Problem

Brian is a freshman in college, and while he hasn't chosen a major yet, he is strongly considering physics. He has always been interested in astronomy and would love to do research in that field some day, perhaps even as an undergraduate.

Unfortunately, Brian is unsure about how to behave around his professors. He is pretty shy and introverted in general; he always has been. He manages to get along well with people he knows, but feels anxious around strangers. And no matter the situation, he doesn't like to draw much attention to himself; in high school, he was voted quietest in his senior class! Brian rarely visits his professors; when he does, he never quite knows how to act. He doesn't feel that he makes a good impression and wishes he could relax more around them. Forming questions isn't the trouble; the more social aspects of the meetings are what trip him up.

Overall Brian's college experience so far has been stressful, although he is relaxing more as the year goes on. He really wants to do research at some point, but he's concerned about his chances. Finding research positions isn't easy, and he worries because he has no professors who he thinks will guide him.

The Solution

Brian will have to get used to interacting with adults at some point or other. Unless he is lucky enough to end up self-employed, he'll have to deal with bosses and advisors in the course of his career. Learning to interact with professors would be great practice. He doesn't need to be frightened of his instructors; they're no less human and no more exalted than the next person. With regard to the social side of interactions, the rules are no different than they are in any other situation with someone unfamiliar. Even so, Brian might not be able to carry off these interactions very comfortably. He isn't awkward only around professors specifically; he finds most social situations intimidating. He may not be able to build relationships with a lot of professors, but he should be able to engage a select few—starting small, with one approachable professor.

Brian is a freshman, so he has a lot of time to meet professors before he has to worry about starting research projects. He should look out for professors who strike him as approachable and less intimidating than the others. Considering all the courses he'll have to take over the next few years, he's virtually guaranteed to have at least one class taught by someone sympathetic. He should then focus on becoming known to this person. He can begin by participating in class or by visiting the professor—whichever one he's most comfortable with. Even though he may feel awkward at first, the more contact he has with his professor, the more comfortable he'll become. Even though he might worry that he isn't making the best impression, he needs to get beyond his fear—starting with nonjudgmental people and building the relationship slowly but continually. Planning what to say in advance is doubly important

for Brian; not only will it ensure that he sounds intelligent and prepared, but it will also give him some extra confidence as he won't
have to think on his feet. He really needs to look out for pleasant-
natured professors—and they *are* out there—and work on gradually building relationships with them. These people will give him
positive feedback and increase his confidence, and maybe offer
him a research position.

4 After Class
Building on Relationships with Good Teachers

So far our concern has been with strategies for learning and excelling during the term, but your work shouldn't stop there. The significance of what happens *after* the course ends isn't always obvious. You work hard for an entire semester and push through final exams—you're exhausted, and the time seems right to set the course behind you. New courses will soon demand your attention, and the upcoming break is first and foremost in your mind. But in forgetting about the semester so quickly, you risk unfair assessments from your teachers. A term's work is too precious and costly to be abandoned; you want to carry its benefits with you. With this in mind, we urge you to make at least one follow-up visit to your teachers after the term ends.

Room for Error

The stress of final exams on students is a secret to no one. What is much less widely known is the pressure that this time period puts on the professors themselves. They're usually given forty-eight to seventy-two hours to complete *all* the grading on final exams and papers and to calculate a final grade for each student. The task is daunting enough even under the best of circumstances.

In large classes, the task can become overwhelming. A professor may also have other commitments to manage at the very same time. He may have other courses to complete. He may be looking forward to his vacation just as much as you are to yours. Ultimately this absurdly compact time frame means that exams and papers will get graded much too quickly and not always accurately.

Grading is much more vulnerable to error than most students can even imagine. In evaluating your essay your instructor may skim your answer, missing important information. He may have an arbitrary ideal essay in mind which yours doesn't match even though you actually said everything you should have. Or when grading problems, your teacher might have misread digits or failed to follow your calculations. His mistake might even be as simple as not having added up your grades from the course or from that single exam correctly. These scenarios are a lot more common than you think possible.

To put these considerations into perspective, suppose that, while taking an exam, you realize that you only have twenty minutes left to complete the second half. You might be able to finish in time, but under these conditions you wouldn't expect to get a high grade. You would probably be susceptible to errors you wouldn't normally make, because of the time pressure. In fact, as you're completing the second half, you would probably focus on just getting through it and not on doing it carefully or perfectly. Who wouldn't adopt this attitude if time didn't permit a better one?

Bearing in mind that your professor is under this kind of time pressure, you need to go over your exam carefully. Unlike exams administered and returned throughout the semester, though, to see your graded final you'll probably need to make a visit to your teacher (see below). If your exam is in order but you still think your grade is not what it should be, set up an appointment with your instructor to discuss it. Perhaps you lost points for something you'd forgotten about (e.g., that quiz you missed when you overslept). But it's also possible that the recorded grades aren't correct. (One of us encountered this situation quite recently. A student had lost 20 points due to a clerical error.) When meeting your teacher, bring your previous papers and exams just in case you need to check. In a nutshell: don't assume your professor has been entirely accurate.

Throughout the semester save your tests and papers as they're returned to you. (In fact, you should make a copy of your papers before submitting them.) For one they're great to study from. They're also your only defense in these circumstances. You might *remember* that you had a higher grade on the first exam than the instructor has in his records but this won't do any good. You'll need proof.

Going Over the Exam

Review carefully every exam and paper to ensure that it was graded accurately. You are the only person who can do this. First, check out every obvious potential screw-up: add up your points, looking carefully at the places where you lost them. If you don't know, ask (nicely) for an explanation of why you lost whatever points you did. Multiple-choice exams are the most foolproof but they're not perfect. Answer keys may contain errors. Your authors have both encountered such errors more than once. Sometimes there are two right answers among the choices or the correct choice is marked wrong. Other tests have more room for error and subjectivity. Don't assume you are wrong unless you understand why. Besides, even if you *are* wrong, get an explanation. Understanding your mistake will help you avoid it in the future.

If there is an error in the answer key, don't rely on another student to find it. Your professor may reward the student who finds the error but not take the trouble to go back over everyone's exam to correct the mistake, especially if grades are already in. Only an extremely conscientious person would go so far. It would take more time than most professors have available. When it comes to uncovering these mistakes, you are your best and only line of defense.

Your defensive strategy doesn't need to be complicated. All you need to do is *ask*. Where did you go wrong in your answer? What more should you have said? This forces your professor to evaluate her own judgment and explain it to you. Your primary concern should be (or at least appear to be) discovering where you went wrong so you can learn from it (see below). But during this discussion, if she has made a mistake, it will come to light. The questions you ask can vary somewhat depending on the type of exam, but the basic idea is the same. For objective tests such as multiple-choice ones your question may not need to be any deeper than just confirming what the correct answer would have been. If the test involves solving problems, you can ask for the solution. Essay and short-answer tests are the trickiest ones to contest, as their grading is subjective. Ask what the professor was looking for in the answer and what you could have done differently. No matter the type of test you absolutely mustn't take an attitude. Chances are the mistake is your own, but it never hurts to check.

Grading inaccuracies aren't always simple mistakes. If you haven't done well on an earlier exam or if you have not displayed—at least according to your teacher's idiosyncratic expectations—the proper enthusiasm for his course, inevitable prejudices settle into his mind. Perhaps he mistook your shyness for indifference—your sitting in the back of the room, your coming in late, your slouching in your seat, or your dressing funny by his standards—who knows? Perhaps all these factors influenced him just as he was about to go through your exam, so he was already disposed to underestimate your work. We don't live in an ideal world, but his subjectivity can be turned to your advantage. (See the next section.) The bottom line is this: after devoting an entire term of hard work to a class, you deserve an evaluation that reflects your accomplishments. Don't let human error get in the way.

Finding errors isn't the only reason for you to go over your exam. Bearing in mind that most students won't ever see their finals, many professors rarely take the time to put anything like detailed comments on them. If, however, your instructor knows to expect a visit from you, he'll pull out your final and go over it beforehand. He'll be forced to evaluate it properly. To encourage his advance preparation, make an appointment before you show up. After all the effort you've put into his course and especially into the final, you deserve a conscientious critique. Did you miss something? Did you finally master a troublesome concept? You should know the answers to these questions. If you plan to take more classes in the field, this information might be extremely important.

Wrong answers aren't necessarily the only ones to attend to. Perhaps you were unsure of some questions you got right. A lucky guess is not comprehension. If you still don't understand, ask for an explanation. Some tests offer a selection of questions to choose from; you could also inquire about ones you didn't answer. Ultimately you're paying to get an education, not to get good grades. Having a better grasp of a subject matter can only benefit you.

Going over the exam is one of the best ways to both protect your grade and get the proper amount and kind of feedback that you deserve. Never assume that it would be pointless to do so or that you don't have the right to get constructive feedback on the final exam or project.

Self-Defense

Your first line of defense against grading problems begins when the class is still in progress. Make yourself known to the teacher. (We've pressed this point throughout the book and have presented a variety of ways you can bring this about.) Some instructors even pull out the tests of those students they know best and grade them first. If a professor has devoted her time to helping a certain student, she will naturally be curious to see how that student has done. Or more often than you might think, she may enter the grading process with no clear standards for measuring success on the exam. She might use answers of those students she deems her best to set the standard for the entire class. So if your exam is among them, it may turn out to be the mold all others must fit, virtually guaranteeing you the highest grade in the class.

The Visit

Going over your exam with your professor requires a visit. As with all your meetings with her, your behavior is important for getting the right results. E-mail her and/or ask in person to set up an appointment, both to give her time to review your final and to ensure she's actually there when you show up. Just say that you would like to look over your final exam or paper. The request doesn't need to be any more complicated than that.

Timing

Try to make your appointments as soon as possible. The ideal time is before the semester ends—just as soon as you know the grades are posted. Of course, this timing isn't always possible; you may be off campus before some grades are posted. If you happen to be staying locally during the vacation period, take advantage of your proximity. Most professors stay around even when the term isn't in session, doing research or taking care of departmental business. As long as you make an appointment, most teachers will be happy to meet with you then.

If you live a long distance from your college, then obviously you won't be able to meet over vacation. In this case, visit your professor as early as possible in the next term. If you leave the visit until midway through the following term, your work won't be fresh in her mind anymore. The feedback that you are likely to get then won't be as helpful or as informative as it could be if you had met earlier.

Don't Ask, Don't Tell

Don't expect to alter your grade unless administrative mistakes have been made. Every year students try pointlessly, seeing if they can get something for nothing. All they do is annoy the faculty. "I only took the course because it's required," "I need a good grade for medical school," "This is the only class I messed up in; all my other grades are better!" are among the hackneyed and hopeless pleas professors hear each and every term. Sometimes these crop up during the term, sometimes only after it's over. They never do any good no matter when they are blurted out. Problems that arise need to be dealt with while the class is still in session—extra time and energy can then be put into clearing up the issues. Once a term is over this opportunity is also over. Remember, if the *professor* is at fault, your grade should be changed; otherwise, there's no chance. Seeking a better grade this way will only end up leaving a bad impression. (Take the first comment above: that the course is required. How would you like to hear from someone you think is your friend that she only hangs out with you because her mother requires her to or because she thought she had to since you two live on the same floor of a residence hall? What good could such a comment possibly do?)

Relationships Revisited

Even if you think your grade is unfair, control your conduct. Don't approach your professor with hostility. You are there as a concerned student. You don't need to regard your teacher as an adversary. You're not there to challenge and confront him but just to see how you did and how you might improve your grasp of the material. (What sweet music to a teacher's ears to hear a student say, "I just want to make sure I've understood the material.")

Another advantage to paying your teacher a visit after the term has ended is that if this is a professor with whom you would like to forge a continuing relationship, then a follow-up meeting is a great first step. It's also an excellent opportunity to ask about any upcoming classes she will be teaching, or to seek advice on choosing other courses in the department or to have her check your list of courses for next term. (As a note on courtesy, never ask a professor to recommend a course for the next semester without asking first if she is teaching one. Her course may not fit your schedule or she may not even be teaching one, but you should always ask.)

Your professor can provide professional feedback that *no one else* on campus can. If you can tell he doesn't give a damn about you and just wants to get the interview over with, have him review the exam, thank him, and say, "So long." But if you sense some connection, go with the flow. He may be someone to take more classes from, to work with later on, or to get a recommendation from. College is too tough to miss an opportunity to get your professor on your side.

Conclusion

A term's worth of hard work deserves more than a hurried evaluation. Letting your final go unexamined leaves you in danger of getting an unfair grade or of learning less than you could have. With this in mind, aim to do the following:

✔ Make an appointment to go over the exam or paper afterward.

✔ Check for inaccuracies in the grading.

✔ Use the visit to build your relationship and get feedback on your work.

Your grade is not likely to be altered by visiting the professor after the semester ends—unless you find an error. But your visit does demonstrate interest and commitment. Students who show a genuine interest in learning impress their teachers as well as build impressive transcripts. Your post-term visit is one more step in nurturing those relationships we have been urging. Your professor can also provide advice on choosing good teachers for the coming term and so a cycle begins.

CASE STUDIES

Andrew's Problem

Andrew didn't do particularly well last semester. He promised himself afterward that he would really concentrate this term and not allow anything to distract him. He mostly succeeded and feels pretty proud of himself. He didn't go out a single weeknight (well, hardly any), and his grades improved markedly. His favorite class this semester was a philosophy class—one on the philosophy of Plato. He worked very hard for it, and really felt that he deserved an A in the course. His midterm score was high, and he did well with the assigned essay. When finals time rolled around, Andrew studied the material and felt prepared to do an outstanding job on the exam, which consisted of one (long) in-class essay. The essay didn't turn out *quite* as well as he had hoped, but he was still reasonably confident and expected an A in the course.

After celebrating the end of the semester (and celebrating it pretty hard) Andrew received his final grades. To his surprise, he only got a B in his Plato class. As his other grades in it had both been As, Andrew was taken aback that his final exam had lowered his grade so significantly. It crossed his mind to go and visit the professor, but the professor had explicitly told the class that he disliked students arguing about their grades. Andrew figured he had just done worse than he had thought on the final, and anyway, a B isn't exactly a bad grade. It still bothered him a bit, though, since he had been so involved in the material and felt he had done better than his final grade reflected.

The Solution

Andrew most definitely needs to pay the professor a visit; he just needs to be careful how his visit comes over. His professor happened to state explicitly that he didn't want students arguing about their grades, but this goes for most all professors, explicitly or otherwise. Approaching the professor to whine for extra points, or demanding to know why you got the grade you did, is a colossally bad idea. What Andrew needs to do is simply find out where he went wrong. If he is interested in the material, he should want to do that anyway; perhaps even though he *thought* he understood the philosophy, he was actually missing important points. This information is important to know even once the class is over.

As this is essentially all Andrew wants to find out, the professor should have no complaints. Andrew should notify the professor that he wishes to look at his exam. While looking at it, he can of course mentally check the grading—see that the points all add up, and that his final grade makes sense in light of his score on his final exam. If there are no clerical errors, he should ask the professor to explain to him material he left out or mishandled. As he hears the explanation, he may well find that the mistakes are his own. If, however, he feels that he did include what the professor thinks he is missing, he needs to bring it up in a nonconfrontational way. He should say that he feels he still doesn't quite understand the difference between what he did write and what he should have written; could the teacher please elaborate more specifically on where he went wrong. This will prompt the professor to look back at his answer, and if the mistake is the professor's own, he'll realize it when he is forced to explain. Andrew just needs to remember that (at least as far as the professor is concerned) he is only there to learn where he went wrong. No matter who made the mistake, Andrew will benefit; he'll learn something if it was his fault, and he'll get the grade he deserves if it was the professor's.

Rebecca's Problem

Rebecca is a freshman and, like many other freshmen, she is still adjusting to college. Living in a dorm, surrounded by friends nearly twenty-four hours a day, she is finding it hard to focus on classwork. There's always something else she'd rather do and somewhere else she'd rather be, so she hasn't been on top of her classes all semester. (At one point she mused whether focusing on school might not come easier if she slept more than four hours each night, but quickly dismissed the idea.)

After her first few exams, she realized that she needed to work harder than she had in high school. Chemistry was giving her the most trouble. Her high school chemistry background had been weak, so parts of the course intended as a review of high school chemistry were new to her. She could name the compounds well enough and understood the concept of moles. (She remembered a mole-day song from high school, which helped her with that!) Unfortunately, she got lost with stoichiometry. Her grade on the first exam was awful, although no surprise.

Rebecca resolved to do better and found a tutor. She raised her grade a *lot* on the second exam (the course gives two midterms and a final), and she was proud of herself. The final is, of course, cumulative. Rebecca is determined to do well on it. She is preparing diligently as she feels this is her chance to prove she can really master the subject.

Rebecca is actually enjoying the class a lot now, and she is even thinking of majoring in chemistry. She's concerned, though, that she might have trouble in higher-level classes if she doesn't have all of the intro course down cold. She would like to know what her weakest areas are, so she can work on them in the future.

The Solution

Adjusting to college is one of the most difficult transitions a person can make. Although Rebecca was having a great social life, she *was* having problems with time management. Her circumstance is understandable and, to a certain extent, predictable. Almost all students have problems during their transition to college. She needs a balance. Resolving to give up her social life to devote herself to studying would not be a practical solution, as it most likely wouldn't last. A better idea would be to allot time to both: perhaps to go out on weekend nights but stay in on weekdays—a compromise she can live with.

That aside, Rebecca still needs to secure some clear and pointed feedback on her chemistry course. Focusing on the final is right for now; she needs to give it all she has. But once the examination is over, she should arrange an after-class trip to her professor. While we advise such a visit no matter the class, it's especially important in this case. Rebecca can ask the instructor for his honest appraisal of her performance. She should begin by explaining her concern; she started off poorly but discovered she really likes chemistry. She is considering majoring in the field, and so could use an honest evaluation of her potential. She should admit that she had problems in the beginning—not in the hope of raising her grade but merely as an explanation of her erratic scores. Asking him to put her first grade into perspective, she should ask him how well he thinks she wound up doing. What should she have focused on more? Does he think she really understood the material? Her professor can point out where she should concentrate next time. Honest evaluations can really help students do better in the future and they are entitled to them after a semester of hard work.

5 The Ins and Outs of Recommendations

Virtually all graduate and professional admissions directors, and most prospective employers, require letters of recommendation. Because they do, every year countless college students find themselves in a bind. They've managed to get through their entire undergraduate career without getting to know a single faculty member who can say anything useful about them. Typically most students end up getting references from the professors who gave them their best grades. But all too often, several terms have passed since they had contact with that professor. Or worse, their greatest successes were in large classes and the professor has no recollection of them as individuals. The professor is only prepared to mention the student's name, class, and grade—facts that their transcripts already reflect.

To see how dire these circumstances can be, imagine that you're the person who screens graduate school applications or who hires recent college graduates. You've narrowed your selection down to two with comparable transcripts: one candidate has recommendations describing her academic achievements, outlining her involvement in the university, and positively evaluating her abilities and personality. The other applicant's recommendations say little more than that she did well in a course and, to the best of the instructor's recollection, was usually punctual. Odds are that you are going to favor the first applicant. For all you know, both may have equal ability, but you, the reviewer, must make your decision on the available information. Now imagine having to choose one out of a hundred applicants! It's nearly impossible to imagine picking a person with perfunctory recommendations.

So what steps can you take to make sure you don't end up with your application in the trash can? Getting recommendations is a complicated business that this chapter will guide you through.

The Importance of Relationships

When getting references, choose professors who know you. We aren't suggesting that you try to develop close social friendships with your professors to receive good letters. First, the odds of success are slim, and second, such relationships are irrelevant to our task. The sorts of relationships we're encouraging are professional, based on a shared interest in the subject matter.

Professors are called on each year to evaluate students who sat as quietly as church mice in the back of the classroom among a hundred other students. The professor might not be able to pick them out of a crowd—or even distinguish them from the wallpaper—so how on earth could she be expected to write positively about them? This kind of namelessness never leads to glowing or informative recommendations.

In life, it's easy to get judged below your actual ability level, but much harder to get judged above it. Our goal isn't to offer you seductive techniques for getting an undeserved endorsement; we just want to improve your chances of getting the recommendation you deserve. Many students are successful throughout college, but wind up with evaluations that don't reflect their achievements. You owe it to yourself to get the references you've earned.

Making Yourself Known

The best strategy for securing terrific recommendations is to take an active interest in your courses. You might be able to get good grades sitting quietly in a classroom, never raising your hand, or making a peep, or attending office hours. But good grades reflect only one small part of your overall college experience.

You need to avoid merging into a sea of other competent students. To make yourself more conspicuous, you don't need to become the class buffoon, cracking jokes or never shutting up. This sort of behavior will not have the desired effect. The most fundamental step—yes, you guessed it!—is class participation. It automatically stimulates your teacher's interest in you. It's also advisable for many other reasons outlined in this book. For getting good references, though, classroom participation alone is not enough.

Visiting an instructor during her office hours can also work wonders. Taking the time to discuss the subject matter with her demonstrates both commitment and interest. In a one-on-one situation, the professor will see your earnest enthusiasm for her class. This kind of interaction forms the basis for a recommendation. Repeated visits reinforce your good start, since your goal is to build a relationship; you want her to remember who you are.

A professor you've sought help from can also be a great choice. Even if your grade from him is not one of your best, you will have demonstrated to him your capacity for hard work and persistence—admirable and essential qualities for success anywhere. Most employers and admissions directors seek people with exactly these traits; you can benefit from letting these people know you possess these qualities. Professors also admire these qualities, and most will be more than happy to describe the difficulty of the course and your dedication to it. A letter like this makes a far better recommendation than one that just states you got an A. Of course, professors can't read minds. If you're having difficulties, you'll need to seek their help in order for them to even act as good witnesses of your efforts.

An Academic Autobiography

Suppose you've done what you can to participate in class. Your instructors are no longer strangers, but it's still unlikely they know *very* much about you. An outstanding recommendation does more than comment on academic performance and good citizenship. You need people who can write you an *interesting* recommendation. For that, of course, they need to know who you are. You want your endorser to point out your *concrete* accomplishments, that you did X, Y, and Z in college and that you did them well. Remember that you need to convey to the admissions/employment directors that you are an outstanding candidate. Fudgey recommendations count little for this, or for anything. Still, few professors ever know or remember the details of their students' college careers. If you've done independent work with one—perfect. But for the rest, there's surely much more to say than they could possibly know or remember. Now, wouldn't it be great if you could somehow write your own recommendation?

Forgery is an option, but more likely to get you incarcerated than admitted or employed. Fortunately, honest and effective options are available. On paper—or better, via e-mail—present your instructor with a (typewritten) intellectual autobiography. The importance of this strategy is hard to overestimate. It shows commitment, provides substance, and may end up *being* the recommendation. Yet students *never* even think of doing this.

Impress the Professor One Last Time

Writing an intellectual autobiography demonstrates for your teacher how well you write, and how dedicated you are to doing your best. His class might have involved little writing, so here's a chance to show your math professor your literary side! Put effort into the letter; have friends read and edit it for you. You want it to be as eloquent, well organized, clear, and informative as it can be. It's a great opportunity; you can put your accomplishments and goals together into a coherent summary. Emphasize your achievements—and let your teacher know which other faculty you've interacted with. Tooting your own horn is a good thing here. Avoid going overboard, but absolutely don't undersell yourself.

Provide Substance

Remember, your goal is to present the teacher with the facts she doesn't know but needs to know. Your professor has only seen you in some circumstances, but you don't want the rest of your achievements to go unnoted. In preparing your autobiography, be sure to give a strong sense of who you are, highlighting achievements and goals. Make a résumé or a list of your activities; start doing this as early as possible—it ensures nothing gets forgotten, and saves time in the end. Just add to the list as you go through college. From your master list choose the activities and accomplishments most relevant to the program or job you're applying for, even if the teacher was not involved in them. You may want to include your transcript or at least an edited list of the courses with grades that you have taken with her and in related disciplines. Describe any related projects (including your thesis if you're writing one).

Graduate and professional schools will be extremely interested to know about your involvement in your chosen field. You should talk about the field—why it interests you, what you have pursued, and why you want to continue your pursuit. Such evidence of genuine interest is just what schools and employers are looking for. Finally, describe your post-college plans as specifically as you possibly can.

Although your professor may not know much about you, you can help him (and yourself) by being very detailed about your accomplishments and plans in your autobiography. This information is invaluable to prospective colleges and employers, but is rarely found in letters of recommendation. Use this to your advantage!

Do-It-Yourself Recommendations

Writing your autobiography is a very savvy thing for the student to do. One huge benefit, we almost hesitate to reveal, is that the teacher will inevitably "borrow" from your letter. Once it is in her hands, she's probably going to use it, citing your accomplishments as you described them in your list. The extent to which they "borrow" will depend on the individual instructor. Still, we specifically suggest e-mailing your letter, since the instructor can easily cut-and-paste your language into her letter. (Another reason to make sure it's well written.) With this in mind, you might want to change the wording around as you hand it to different professors. If they strike you as likely to "borrow," make sure you do this.

Keeping Your Options Open

Your self-summary will provide context for your reference, but choosing the right professor is still most important. You probably won't need more than about three recommendations for any position (sometimes fewer), but don't restrict yourself to three professors. When the time for references rolls around, you should be in a position to pick and choose whom to ask. Having more choices than you need gives you insurance. Any number of problems might arise. The professor that you want to ask may be unavailable; maybe he's left the university or is on leave that term; maybe he belongs to a department irrelevant to your future plans (more on that later), and so on. Even when you don't face any of these irritating problems, you will and should be able to choose whom you believe is most informed and well disposed to write you the best letter. By focusing on a select few early on, you may miss the opportunity to form better relationships with others later. There's never a good reason to focus too narrowly anyway; exposure to many professors can hardly be damaging, and almost always has the opposite effect.

The Selection Process

Providing you have quite a few professors to choose from, the time will arrive to decide whom to ask for a letter. While the most important criterion is your instructors' impression of you, you should keep in mind other crucial factors.

The Relevance of the Discipline

If you're applying to a graduate program in a specific field, recommendations from faculty members outside that area of study are nearly worthless. Why students don't understand this fact is beyond us. Why would an admissions director for a physics department want to know what your history professor thinks of you as a physicist or vice versa? The skills set that goes into making a terrific historian may not transfer to a career in physics. If the two disciplines are closely related, however, getting a recommendation from one might work for the other. If you plan to study computer science, for example, a recommendation from a mathematician can have value. But if you plan to study math, a recommendation from a musician likely won't. Even if the fields are related, a letter from someone actually in the field is almost always preferable. The graduate program to which you are applying is interested in your abilities in the field. Your abilities in other areas are beside the point.

Applying for a career position or graduate school is very

different from applying to college as a high school senior. Most likely, you got recommendations from a variety of high school teachers or guidance counselors, maybe even making a special point of getting a letter from a humanities teacher, another from a math/science teacher, and so on. You wanted to show that you were well rounded and capable in a variety of fields. Your decision was wise back then, but it is inadvisable now. Graduate schools only need to know about your potential in your chosen discipline.

The options are looser if you're applying to a professional school—law school, medical school, an MBA program, or even for a job in "the real world." But an instructor's discipline should still be relevant to the abilities needed for the job. For example, if you're applying to law school, recommendations from a political scientist or a philosopher are more relevant than one from a French teacher, especially if the professors in question talk about your critical reasoning skills. If you're applying for an accounting position, business and math instructors are more relevant than psychology instructors, especially if the former are prepared to discuss your technical ability, since this ability is essential in this field. Your recommendations should show that you are more than a good citizen; they should show that you have the necessary skills and talents to perform well in your future profession.

The Prominence of the Instructor

The instructor's professional status can also be an important consideration. If you're in the classroom of a distinguished academic and you want to attend a graduate program in her area of research, then of course you want to obtain a strong letter from her. It can make *all* the difference. Graduate programs at different universities are often related to each other like an extended family. Someone distinguished in one program clues in a crony from another that you are a promising student, and then—boom!—you are on your way to graduate school with a full fellowship. Don't underestimate the power of connections.

We aren't saying you're lost if you don't have an eminent professor writing you a letter, that you have zero chance of getting in a graduate program with financial support. Distinction is not necessary, but if your professor has wide acclaim in her field, a word from her will obviously carry weight. Just as you are trying to develop a relationship with your teachers over the course of your college career, your teacher has been developing relationships with her colleagues during her entire career. These considerations are probably most important for graduate schools, but are still relevant to other aspirations. A political scientist might be well connected to a particular law school's faculty, making a recommendation from her very valuable for getting into that law school. That's what you're banking on when you ask her for a letter of recommendation.

But even when these luminaries aren't available at your college, you should always aim to get recommendations from professors, particularly those who are well established. Choose full professors over associate professors and associate professors over assistant professors, full-time over adjuncts. (See the Afterword.) Adjunct instructors and graduate students should be your last resort. They're unlikely to have acquired the reputation or connections that can help you along. Whether it's true or not, readers will assume that they are easier to impress than hard-bitten professors are. A recommendation from one of these just won't (and shouldn't) count for as much as one from a full professor.

Finding Someone Who Cares

Choosing a prominent professor in an appropriate discipline isn't your only goal. Ideally you want a professor who actually cares about your future. Have your antennae up for faculty members who take a genuine interest in helping their students find the right path after graduation. Some faculty members take a universal interest in all their students; they are well worth finding. Some lack a universal interest, but may take an interest in a particular student. These professors do exist and are on your campus. Find them. Ask around—they'll probably be known.

When you're trying to decide on professors, ask yourself if he has ever shown interest in your work. Has he ever asked about which other courses you are taking? Does he ask you about your plans after graduation? You should probably be able to tell from the beginning whether he has any interest in you. You can tell straight off in a social situation whether an acquaintance cares about you. You are able to discern the subtle signs; we don't need to point them out for you. Be sensitive in the same way when dealing with potential recommenders.

Two professors can have an equal impression of your abilities and have equally much to write about you, but one will produce a much better letter than the other. You have no control over this difference, except that you can choose which one you ask. Ask yourself, "Will this professor put herself out to help me?" Some instructors will bend over backward to assist their students; others can hardly be bothered to attend class. Pay attention to how your professor teaches. Does she seem to spend a lot of time preparing? Is she readily available for office hours? She should *want* to interact with you. These are good signs that she cares about her students and is happy to help them out. Remember, you want a person who is willing to put a lot of time and energy into your letter, not someone who will just hammer out a few lines.

Timing

Like anyone else, professors tend to forget the people they knew once but haven't met recently. And don't forget that the paradigm of a forgetful person is the absent-minded professor! So you shouldn't be asking for a recommendation two whole years after your last contact with your professor. You may have done everything right: participated, talked to him after class, done well in the course, and so on. But a few years later, regardless of the quality of your performance, he will probably not remember very much, so you won't get the recommendation you deserve.

One obvious solution is to get recommendations from those professors you're currently, or recently, in contact with. Besides ensuring you haven't been forgotten, this solution has another advantage: people tend to mature over the years (most of us, anyway). You want to be evaluated on how you are now, not as you were a year or two ago. (One of us once asked for a letter of recommendation from a professor he had studied with as a freshman. Needless to say, that recommendation was poor. Years later, the professor brought up the incident and apologized. That student, now himself a professor, said it was his own fault; he shouldn't have asked for that letter on so flimsy a relationship.)

Sometimes, though, you may find a professor early on that you get along with very well, and so from whom you would very much like a recommendation. In this case you should keep the lines of communication open. Drop by to chat from time to time; send him an e-mail to say hello, and keep him informed of your progress. Or just let him know you are thinking about him. (Don't be a nuisance, though. Moderation in all things!) See if he's planning to teach anything else you might take, whether he can recommend another course, or how he feels about the courses you are currently taking. These easy sorts of communications enhance the chances that he won't forget you (and can help the relationship along).

Alternatively you might, early on, request a letter from a current professor. Proximity works particularly well for students who have done well in a course—perhaps one not even in their major—but are intending to go on to, say, law school, medical school, or on the job market in the field. In these circumstances you might only need a brief letter indicating just how well you did in a particular class, but it's still a bad idea to wait. There's no reason not to pick up a letter or two as you go along, especially if your performance in the professor's class is important to your plans. You always have the option to not use the letters. You won't have the option to get a good letter, though, once a few years have passed.

Confidentiality

Picking and choosing which letters to send would be the ideal situation for a student. You could ask any number of professors for a recommendation, then select the best ones. Unfortunately, many graduate programs don't take recommendations too seriously unless the student has waived her right to read them. The professor mails the letter without the student's ever seeing it, so picking and choosing is not an option. (As a side note, you should always provide the professor with a stamped addressed envelope he can mail the letter in.)

The admissions people are concerned that professors will feel pressured to write positive though insincere comments if students can read their letters. Thus good recommendations count for little if they aren't confidential. With this in mind, you should be prepared to waive your right to see your letters; all the more reason to be sure that you are asking the right people.

How and What to Ask

Once you have selected the lucky few you plan to ask for a recommendation, the question remains how to ask them. They're probably busy, so you must allow a fair amount of time for them to write your evaluation. Asking them a day before it needs to be mailed will only result in annoyance and a rushed job.

Assuming that they already know you well, and that they like you, you need only send a quick e-mail. With others, even though you have participated in class and attended office hours, you may still feel unsure of how well they know you or of their opinion regarding you. In this case make the request carefully. Ask *in person* eyeball to eyeball about the possibility of the professor's writing a recommendation. There are several reasons for doing so. First, your presence assures that the professor remembers who you are. Names are more easily confused than faces. It's also more polite. Meeting in person gives you an opportunity to talk for a few minutes, to remind her how terrific you are. Perhaps more importantly, though, it gives you an opportunity to gauge just how highly this professor actually ranks you. You would have to be totally blind, deaf, and dumb not to recognize that a professor has *no* interest in writing you a good letter of recommendation, based simply on her reaction to your request. Trust us, you can smell complete indifference, aversion, or reluctance. If you detect resistance, politely say good-bye and just forget to send this professor your recommendation form. Even if there isn't a form, they don't know that. Say you'll send them it, then do no more.

More likely than not, you wouldn't (and shouldn't) be requesting a recommendation from someone who has zero interest in your future. If you are, you're making a mistake, and we hope we can prevent it. Suppose you have done your homework (both literally and figuratively), and you're about to ask for a letter of recommendation, which could be one of the most intimidating experiences of your life. Make sure you articulate your request in just the right way. You are *not* going to receive a lot of second chances. You must ask your professor whether she can write a *strong* recommendation for you for such-and-such a program.

We urge you to use the word *strong* or words to that effect because your professor, when asked in person, might feel cornered into writing. He might agree to write you a letter, knowing in advance that his letter will be weak or lukewarm. Or, he might feel that writing letters is part of his job, so he shouldn't refuse to do so. If he agrees and goes ahead out of a sense of duty, you will probably wind up with a poor letter. Don't take that risk, especially if you aren't sure how highly he ranks you or how well he remembers you. However, if you ask your professor whether he can write you a *strong* letter of recommendation, he'll give you an honest answer. Your language will drive home to him how important a letter from him is to you and your future. You will force him to show his hand. He can't agree and then write you a poor one without having lied, which is very unlikely. You may be hurt if he refuses to write you a strong recommendation. But you're better off to be hurt by his words then and there than by his deeds when it counts. Go home afterward (should he decline) and have a good cry. Then get up and try someone else. You mustn't forget that once your teacher's letter is on its way to admissions directors or job recruiters, you no longer have control over your own destiny, at least not in regard to these programs. So, force an answer from the professor when you ask him. Can he write you a *strong* letter of recommendation?

We apologize if our advice is blunt. Nobody said the process was going to be easy. Our aim is to ensure you your best shot. The costs are high enough to call for boldness.

Conclusion

Even in the best of circumstances, it isn't easy to secure a letter that does justice to all your abilities and accomplishments. Our advice, if followed, optimizes your chances of securing good and useful references. Choosing the right person is absolutely essential. It's never too early in a college career to start thinking about recommendations; build strong relationships from day one. When the time comes, you'll be in the ideal situation to choose the very best references, bearing in mind the advice presented here:

✔ Find instructors who know who you are.

✔ Be prepared with an academic autobiography.

✔ Make sure their disciplines are relevant to your plans.

✔ Try to find the highest-ranking people you can.

✔ Don't procrastinate until years after the class ends.

✔ Ask in person for a *strong* recommendation.

Recommendations are very important for post-graduation plans. Make sure that the letters you secure accurately reflect your abilities and accomplishments. After all you've done, you deserve it.

CASE STUDIES

Maria's Problem

All her life Maria has known that she wants to be a doctor. She worked hard in high school to get into a good college and has continued to work hard throughout her first year of school, taking the standard required courses. She's now starting her second year and wants to begin preparing for medical school applications. Maria knows you don't have to be a biology major to go to medical school. In fact medical schools like to accept classes representing a range of majors. For this reason, being a biology major can sometimes even be a disadvantage, or so Maria has heard. With this in mind, as she has always enjoyed English literature, she decides to major in English.

She recognizes the skills required to do well in an English major are not those needed to do well in medical school. As a pre-med student, however, she is taking the core science courses—biology, chemistry, math, and physics. Maria has been an active participant in her classes and has a good rapport with her professors. She is sure she can find professors from these fields to comment on her, but these requirements won't extend past this year. Recommendations based on sophomore year don't seem like the best idea.

The Solution

As English is her major, Maria is right to worry about getting a recommendation from within the sciences. She should check with her college's pre-med advisor to make sure English is a good choice, and that she is taking enough science classes—relying on rumors about what's required isn't a good idea. That aside, she will presumably have to write some sort of senior thesis in literature; there is no reason why she can't get a letter from that advisor. But she should also take care to secure recommendations from faculty in a scientific field. A person can have facility with the English language—nothing to be sneezed at—but be a dunce when it comes to science, and vice versa. She needs to let the medical schools know she can handle both. As she has already developed some rapport with professors from her core classes, she should aim to stay in contact with them. She should also request recommendations immediately after the courses are finished. (In this case though, she will lose the chance to have the letters reflect that she has matured throughout college.) She might even consider spending a summer doing research with one of her science professors, perhaps, so as to build an even stronger rapport, and also to gain experience in a science lab. If her major and other requirements permit, she would do well to take further science courses, doing a few in her last years to give her the contact she needs, to underline her scientific abilities.

Tom's Problem

Tom never really worked in college. Sometimes he went to class; sometimes he didn't. Sometimes he did his assignments; sometimes he didn't. Enjoying college a lot, Tom disregarded his future. After all, college is supposed to be the best years of your life, and Tom had no intention of wasting them studying.

He's now reached his senior year and just recently had a wake-up call. He had the idea that he could go to graduate school in psychology, but he hadn't done much to actualize this end. His girlfriend, Susan, is also planning to go on in psychology and has started getting on his case about applications. She pointed out to him the other day that he is not in a good situation: while his Graduate Record Examination (GRE) scores aren't too bad, his Grade Point Average (GPA) is not so high, and he knows virtually no professors. His chances of getting into a good graduate program are not good. Susan's blast actually stunned him. Until then he had been able to goof off yet continue to delude himself into thinking a graduate school would accept him. What is he supposed to do?

The Solution

Tom has landed himself in an awkward position. (Susan should have been around to give her wake up call years ago!) But all is not lost, although he will have to change his plans. If he is determined to go to graduate school in psychology, he needs some help from a psychologist—academic, not clinical, that is. His chances of getting accepted to a halfway decent program look slim as things stand. (Of course, he can get accepted *somewhere*. Some programs will take anyone with enough money.) He should plan to wait at least a year, perhaps two, before applying. During those years, he needs to find a sympathetic professor to help him out. Finding someone won't necessarily be easy, but it can be done. When all is said and done, Tom is still only twenty-one years old. If he should have to postpone his graduate studies until, say, he is twenty-three, nothing significant has been lost.

Tom needs to go to his professors and explain his situation. He needs to be frank. He was immature and messed up but he has changed. Many instructors will be unwilling to help him, but with some luck some will be. Once he has found those people, he needs to work out a plan. He should aim to do some independent work with them—probably in their labs or clinics—and perhaps audit their classes. He needs to work for them in some capacity, since he needs to prove his commitment; just hanging around auditing classes will not do that. Obviously he will have to work hard, but at the end of it he will probably be able to get admitted into a graduate program. Although his GPA leaves much to be desired, strong letters of recommendation—especially ones describing his newfound determination—will most likely suffice to get him accepted.

Christina's Problem

Christina has been interested in how the mind works since she was a child. When her little brother was born, she was puzzled and fascinated by how he developed and was able to acquire language. When she got to college, she discovered cognitive science, which addresses the questions she has always wanted to answer, and immediately fell in love with the subject. Now that she is graduating, she wants to continue studying the subject, and so has decided to pursue a Ph.D. in cognitive psychology. She is specifically interested in the mechanisms that underlie thought, and would like to write her dissertation on the topic.

Christina has participated in a lot of activities, including volunteering as a tutor, playing on the soccer team, and joining the school Cognitive Science Club. The graduate programs in psychology all require letters of recommendation, and she wants to make sure she gets good ones. She wants to send one of her professors the following letter, intended as an academic autobiography, but isn't sure if it's saying all it should.

Dear Professor Kastner,

I really enjoyed your class when I took it, and I got an A. It was very interesting. I think I want to go to graduate school in Cognitive Psychology, so hopefully you will be able to write me a recommendation. I would really appreciate it if you could.

I have been active in a lot of things in my college years. For example, I was on the soccer team for two years, which taught me a lot. I really think that attending college has let me grow as a person and I have really matured. One of the most important things is to remember that we all should give back to the community, and I have tried to do this through volunteer work.

My grades have been generally good and I made the Dean's List a few times. I am looking forward to meeting new challenges at graduate school and in life in general. I know I am capable of facing up to these.

Sincerely,

Christina Hudson

The Solution

Christina's letter is definitely not going to cut it. Little in her letter could be used as a basis for an outstanding recommendation. She only cites one example of her activities, and it is not even the most relevant example. She should also pay more attention to her style—the letter reads poorly.

Christina needs to stay clear of clichés about growing as a person and giving back to the community. Such comments are irrelevant, overused, and boring. The graduate school needs to know about her prior involvement with cognitive science and her specific future plans, not about how she wants to "face new challenges." She ought to have written her letter as though she were writing her own recommendation; only poor recommendations throw around banal phrases.

The letter also begins as if it is a *request* for a recommendation. This request should have been made in person, face to face, and the letter should only have been sent as a follow-up. A far better letter, to be sent both as hard copy and e-mail, would run as follows:

Dear Professor Kastner,

I appreciate your taking the time to discuss my future plans, and I want to thank you for agreeing to write me a letter of recommendation. As you know, I am applying to graduate programs in cognitive psychology. I am especially interested in the cognitive mechanisms that underlie the workings of the mind. The various neural net models that have been proposed all face deep troubles, and I believe these troubles are fatal. Any successful cognitive model must incorporate symbolic processing; the question is to what degree. I plan to address this question in my graduate studies, and hope to continue to address it for as long as it remains unanswered.

At this university I have been involved in a variety of activities as an undergraduate, including the Cognitive Science Club. I gave a presentation to the club in the fall in which I discussed the current debate over the nature of concepts. Although the theory-theory of concepts is still widely accepted, many of the arguments supporting it are flawed, and I concluded in favor of Jerry Fodor's atomistic approach. Given how much preparation my talk required, I was pleased that the other members of the club received it well.

In addition to my academic pursuits, I have been a member of the soccer team for two years. I also volunteer as a tutor and I recently received the Reginald M. Harrington Award for Community Service.

I've attached my transcript so that you can see my level of academic pursuit and success, including my grade in your course. I have completed my cognitive science major with a GPA of 3.39, and have been on the Dean's List three times. I believe I am ready for graduate school, and I hope that you will be able to write me a strong letter of recommendation.

You need only write one letter to be sent to the Office of the

Dean of Students at ___. They will forward your letter in my general packet to each program to which I apply. I intend to apply to the following programs: ___. If you think that I shouldn't apply to a particular program or that I ought to apply to one I did not mention, please contact me at ___.

Thanks once again for your time. I will keep you posted on my progress as I hear from the various programs.

Sincerely,
Christina Hudson

Afterword
Why Bad Teaching Persists

It's hard to pinpoint just how it all begins—why it is that students, semester in and semester out, wind up stuck with uninspired teaching, even at colleges where good teaching is the norm. When you think about it, a college is a business a lot like any other business. It has a budget with a surplus or a deficit at the end of each year. It screens and hires and evaluates personnel. Nevertheless, conspicuously bad classroom teachers are employed by every college and university. Why isn't there better quality control? Why aren't bad classroom teachers weeded out, as inferior employees in other consumer markets are? Perhaps some of the problem lies with the *tenure* system. It's hard to get rid of a bad classroom teacher once she is tenured. We are not saying that the current tenure system lacks merit. Many terrific reasons exist for maintaining it, and the odds are very high that it will continue. Indeed, we wrote this book precisely because we realize that the tenure system in the United States isn't about to change any time soon; and we applaud that. We thought students could use advice about how to survive a system that, even with an abundance of admirable features, still cannot guarantee you an adequate teacher, much less a stellar one.

You don't need to read a full-length treatise on tenure, though. Even if interesting in itself, as both a historical and a political document, it is not going to help you find better teachers. However, what might be useful and would certainly help you avoid bad teaching is a brief sketch of the academic structure of a normal university. This Afterword is designed to bring you up to speed quickly.

Rank

Graduate Students

Many universities have both undergraduate and graduate students. Graduate students have undergraduate degrees, mostly from other institutions. They normally apply to a graduate department (e.g., philosophy, physics, English, history, or biology) during their senior year of college. If accepted, sometimes they may be awarded financial aid in the form of a fellowship or a teaching assistantship. Teaching assistants help professors in large lecture courses by leading recitation sections, taking lab sessions, or grading exams and papers. Eventually they may teach a course independently, almost always a low-level "service course," for example, the "101" introductory course in a subject matter. These introductory courses are called "service courses" because they contribute to the general education of all students. Departments use these courses to build up their enrollment figures—their body counts. These counts play a major role in determining future departmental funding; for example, how much money a department will receive for its graduate students, how many professorial positions the department is entitled to, and what sort of operating budget it has. Naturally, the department wants to keep these figures as high as it can.

Most senior faculty teach higher-level courses, partly because the service courses are too elementary. You do the arithmetic. If a faculty member is, say, fifty years old, then she has most likely been teaching for twenty-five years, at two terms a year. If she were to teach the same service course each year, that would add up to her having taught that course perhaps as many as fifty different times, not counting those times she may have taught or assisted in these courses as a graduate student or those summers or intersessions when she may have taught to pick up a few extra bucks. How many times can a person listen to herself going through the same introductory subject matter, which tends to be fixed, changing very little from year to year?

Even for those senior faculty who want to teach a service course—this has happened several times to one of us—a department head or the director of undergraduate studies might try to dissuade him. She may need him for higher-level courses, since they too must be taught, and she may feel more comfortable throwing a neophyte graduate student into a service course than into a course of advanced studies. You can see the reasoning here. Graduate students are less prepared to teach advanced courses. However, "being more prepared" needn't mean "being well prepared."

This system has a very perverse consequence: in the elementary courses that first expose you to the subject matter, you are more likely to be placed in the hands of someone just a couple of years ahead of you. While he may be more likely to empathize with your situation, his experience in that subject matter may not even surpass your own by more than a mere term or two.

To make matters worse, academic departments rarely organize programs designed to teach graduate students *how* to teach. This deficiency has far-reaching consequences. The graduate student teaching you probably hasn't been taught to teach your course. Even worse, your full professors likely did not have any pedagogical training either. An undergraduate entering the classroom has no guarantee that his instructor is able to teach effectively.

Here's another problem. Not only are graduate students not taught how to teach, the odds are high that no one will seriously supervise, evaluate, or help them to improve their teaching. Normally, when graduate students are completing their degrees and beginning to seek jobs as professors, their advisors will comment on their teaching qualifications. These comments are usually based on student evaluations and on hearsay from undergraduate students. In some cases on-site (but announced) visits to the graduate student's class may occur. But these are hardly fail-safe detectors of good or bad teaching. Rarely will an awful teacher, whether a professor or a graduate student, be required to attend a seminar or given constructive help. He is told briefly to do this or do that. That's the end of it. He may acquire a reputation for not being a good teacher but usually such tales are told in the context of praise! "He's not a teacher—he's more of a researcher." (Get this—sometimes it will be said of inferior graduate students as a way of indicating that they are inferior, "Oh, well, at least he can teach.")

Do you still doubt how undervalued teaching is inside our senior colleges and therefore why it's so important to use every clue you can to find good teachers?

We aren't trying to depress you, but to make you aware that many graduate students are not taught to teach. Some are naturals, some work hard, prepare more, are bright, know about the subject, and so on. You should, of course, try to identify them, and we hope that our advice will help you in your search. But we also hope you are better motivated than you were before, now that you know the odds you're up against.

Instructors/Assistant Professors

After completing a graduate education, the name of the game is to get a job, often at another institution of higher learning. If a graduate student has completed her dissertation, often a book-length manuscript written during her last year(s) of graduate study, she will apply for various jobs and, with more than a little luck, she might land one. (When you think about how many students are attending college these days, it's surprising how few graduate students there are and how even fewer of them actually go on to practice university teaching. Could it have something to do with lagging salaries? Our cynicism knows no bounds.)

If a graduate student completed her degree before she begins her new job, she is usually awarded an *assistant professorship*. If she has all but her dissertation done (ABD), she will be awarded an *instructorship*. (The difference between the two is mostly a matter of salary.) Usually, the university places a time limit on how long a graduate student has to complete her dissertation before her contract is voided. Or she may be given a temporary contract until she completes her degree.

Normally, an assistant professor is appointed for three years, with a possible renewal for another three years. Renewal is almost automatic. A department has to harbor real doubts about the potential of a junior faculty member before letting her go at the first renewal stage.

When the second three-year term draws to a close, an assistant professor is evaluated to determine whether the department wants to keep her as a *tenured* member of the department—usually designated as an *associate professor*. The prospect of termination after the sixth year of employment virtually guarantees the assistant professor's unbridled enthusiasm and limitless commitment during the trial period. They are fighting for their academic careers. Theoretically, after six years, if the assistant professor has failed to meet the criteria for tenure and promotion established by her senior colleagues, she can be denied tenure or, less euphemistically, fired. Then she will either change careers or seek an assistant professorship at another institution.

The first six years of one's professional academic career can be tough. A junior faculty member is expected to be a model colleague. This usually means he is expected to participate in more than his share of departmental duties and committee work, publish a great deal, make a name for himself in his chosen field of specialization, and—we say this almost as an afterthought—to establish himself as a good teacher.

As we noted above, assistant professors typically receive no teaching instruction. An assistant professor might, if courageous, ask a colleague how she teaches a certain course, but this kind of request is rare. In addition, assistant professors usually have heavier teaching loads than their senior colleagues do, and they are assigned to more introductory service courses. So, lower-level courses are taught, by and large, either by junior faculty members fresh out of graduate school with little or no prior teaching experience or by graduate students themselves. (There is also a category of part-time lecturers [PTLs] to which we'll return below.)

None of these built-in deficiencies means that assistant professors (or even graduate students) can't teach or even be superior teachers. Younger faculty are often more eager and enthusiastic than the seasoned pros. We aren't telling you to avoid them; we are merely emphasizing the need for caution.

Tenured Faculty (Associate/Full Professors)

On the assumption that a faculty member is awarded tenure, he will likely be promoted to the position of associate professor. The title is irrelevant; it's the tenure that counts. This advancement spells a percentage salary raise, enhanced status in the department and the profession, lower blood pressure, and perhaps a slightly better teaching schedule, better courses at better times and days. The real boon from tenure, though, is that the tenured faculty member cannot be fired, short of being caught doing something egregiously irresponsible or illegal. Although this is rare, should a tenured faculty member choose to, he might never publish another article or book. He might never perform another experiment or apply for another grant or ever act as the advisor of a graduate student. A standard contractual agreement is likely to include a clause that a tenured faculty member is supposed to teach a certain number of courses, attend departmental meetings regularly, hold office hours, and that's about it. There are few sanctions against lousy teaching. A tenured faculty member can't get fired for being a bad teacher. In effect the university is stuck with its tenured faculty members. Indeed, without a mandatory retirement age, they are literally stuck with them for life.

The original reason for instituting tenure was to protect faculty members' academic freedom—so that they cannot be fired for voicing eccentric or unpopular views or for engaging in research that is out of the mainstream. The academy, after all, is supposed to be the temple of learning. Learning cannot take place in an environment in which the faculty fear their views might land them in the soup.

In all fairness, professors almost never stumble and fall into a coma just after receiving tenure. Most continue on their merry ways, publishing and doing whatever they can to further their careers. After all, they chose their professions because they liked the subject matter. Besides, careerism rules as much in the academy as it does in other professions.

After another five years or so pass, a faculty member can be put up (by herself or her department) for another promotion, this time from associate tenured professor to the rank of full professor. Five years is normally the minimum, but there is no specific time. Some faculty retire as associate professors. Withholding promotion to full professor is supposed to be a stick to hold over the heads of potential academic freeloaders. Peer pressure works, too. It's hard to be on a quasi-permanent vacation while your peers are pushing their careers forward. And, lastly, colleagues are pretty good at ferreting out before tenure who is likely to become an albatross after tenure.

Why do you need to know any of this? Not much hangs in the balance of whether you wind up with an associate or full professor as your teacher, though the full professors tend to be the more distinguished members of the department, and so, as we noted in the chapter on recommendations, they tend to be better connected. Their word carries more weight. More than their distinction, though, the tenured faculty have longevity as stable members of the institution. They tend to be better informed about the workings of the university, and so they can be an excellent source of advice and information about who else is a good teacher and about career choices. So if you are presented with perfectly equal choices between a graduate student, assistant professor, associate professor, or full professor— and they really are equal choices—you should opt for the most senior first and work your way down.

Part-Time Lecturers

A whole other category is the part-time lecturer or adjunct. He is someone employed by the university to teach a single course or set of courses. His contract is usually for a single semester; he is not on a track toward tenure, and he cannot vote in departmental decisions. Pretty much he has to take whatever is thrown his way by the director of undergraduate studies, whose job is to ensure that a full range of courses is offered each term.

A director is obliged to field and staff a certain number of courses. Often he finds himself without enough faculty or graduate students to cover them all. So when push comes to shove, he may have to find someone to teach an odd course here or there. We do not want to lay down any hard rules about the quality of PTLs. Some people love to teach and are prepared to teach well regardless of how little they are paid. Especially in small departments a PTL might provide a different but needed perspective. But PTLs receive a fraction of what others are paid, including graduate students, to teach. They are usually given the most overcrowded courses, during the most undesirable periods, on the worst days.

They are not treated well and consequently might feel little or no allegiance to the institution or department. They usually do *not* have offices on campus—certainly not permanent ones—so their office hours might be irregular. They are unlikely to be on campus on those days they are not teaching—they have no reason to be—so they are unlikely to be as available as a full-time faculty member. They often do not know which course they are going to teach until the last moment, sometimes the day the class begins. Did you ever notice that when you pre-register it sometimes says "taught by staff"? At the very late date that the preregistration course book was put together, the undergraduate director still did not know who was going to teach that course. Most full-time teachers know at least a half-year in advance—sometimes longer—which courses they will be teaching. So "staff" usually means teaching assistants or PTLs. Once assigned a course, PTLs have little control or room for creativity. Often they don't even get to choose the assigned books.

None of this, we repeat, is meant to put down the PTLs, but it is a warning not to take their classes if you can avoid them, not because they are likely to be poorer teachers, but because the deck is so stacked against them. (Needless to say, PTLs are usually poor choices for references.)

Conclusion

The quality of teaching varies widely within universities and within departments. But understanding the ranking system gives you great advantages when registering for classes and when choosing whom to ask for a recommendation. As a rule of thumb, always opt for the highest ranked person. This factor does not, of course, supercede any other information you have collected on an instructor's teaching abilities in the ways that we have already suggested. Good judgment always needs to be exercised. If you are really interested in the subject matter, you may find an equally enthusiastic junior faculty member has persuaded the fogies in the department to allow her to teach a new course—and you'll enjoy a memorable semester.

A Guide to Academic Vocabulary

Advisors

At many institutions, first-year students are assigned an advisor. This advisor may be a faculty member who has agreed to counsel students, or someone specifically employed to do so. Even if you are not automatically assigned an advisor, your college most likely has some counseling services available for you. Check at your academic service office for information, or contact the dean of first-year students.

Until you've officially declared a major, your advisor will probably not be affiliated with the department of your major. Nonetheless, academic advisors can be great sources of information. They know their way around the intimidating university bureaucracy, and can give you vital information about your university's registration policies, required courses, and other college-specific technicalities. Find out from your advisor which courses you should be taking at this stage, and how you can best fulfill your general college requirements. If you're thinking of taking a double major, he should be able to tell you how feasible that will be—for example, if you'll need to take an extra year or semester. If you're pretty certain about your career goals but are undecided about your major, your advisor may be able to suggest the best majors for you given your plans.

Once you've declared a major, you should aim to find an advisor within that department. Many colleges assign faculty advisors within majors, but if yours doesn't, don't give up. With the strategies in this book you can always find an unofficial advisor. At some colleges students are even allowed to approach a faculty member within their major department and ask to be taken on as an advisee. The department might also have an undergraduate director who can help you with your questions.

An advisor within your department is helpful in various ways. She can give you specific information about the best ways to fulfill the major requirements. If you're unsure about your career plans she can tell you what career options are available to people graduating with a degree in the subject. She can also provide you with inside information about research projects, outstanding courses, and other opportunities within your major.

When approaching an advisor—whether he is a general academic advisor or a faculty advisor in your major—your behavior should be much the same as when visiting a professor during office hours (see Chapter 3). Make an appointment beforehand and, most importantly, come prepared with a list of questions. As questions come up during the term, write them down and keep the list. That way, you're prepared enough to get the information you need. We recommend visiting your advisor at least once a semester, preferably shortly before you register for classes. Have him look over your course list and give you feedback on your choice of courses (and professors). Are there any other classes you should be taking at this stage? Are there any particularly good classes you're missing out on? You can also take the opportunity to review your progress so far, checking that your grades are high enough for you to meet your goals and that your classes and activities are letting you develop the skills you need.

If your advisor gives you information that contradicts other things you've heard, be sure to check up on it by looking for written information (try online) or asking someone else. Most universities provide undergraduate catalogues, which are often available online as well as in print. The catalogue will have information about the college's official policies, and we recommend looking through it before meeting with your advisor to make sure all your facts are straight. As a rule of thumb, general academic advisors should be trusted for information about university procedures, while faculty advisors should be trusted for information about their departments, for example, about good courses. General academic advisors may lack accurate information about specific courses or about the details of your major; faculty advisors often know nothing about bureaucratic processes. (Ask any department secretary to what extent professors can be trusted with their own paperwork, let alone anyone else's.) If in doubt, always get a second opinion.

Course Levels

Within a department courses are ranked according to how advanced they are. The exact nature of this ranking varies from college to college, although many places use the 100–400 level system. Courses are divided into four categories, supposedly into freshman (100), sophomore (200), junior (300), and senior (400) level courses. This is quite misleading. While younger students typically take more low-level courses (often called intro-level courses) and upperclassmen take more advanced ones, the division is fairly loose. Certainly you shouldn't limit yourself to a particular level of course based on class year.

No matter the system your college uses to rank courses, bear in mind that the system is probably pretty vague. The actual difficulty level of a course ultimately depends on the instructor. We've both known introductory classes that were more challenging than advanced ones, even within the same department. In fact, some departments make their intro-level courses very difficult on purpose, so as to "weed out" (read: discourage) students who aren't wholly committed to the discipline. This is especially true in natural science or math courses. In short, don't assume that advanced courses are always more difficult or more work than lower level ones.

Of course, lower-level courses are often prerequisites for more advanced ones, that is, you have to take the intro classes before you can take the higher-level ones. Introductory courses also offer overviews of the subject in ways that the more specific courses can't. Unfortunately, intro classes are often taught by less experienced faculty (see the Afterword), and can turn students off from the subject. Take particular care in finding good teachers for these classes; besides, you'll have more choices than with upper-level courses as there are either usually multiple sections of intro classes, or these courses are taught more frequently. (Upper-level courses tend to be taught less frequently— check their pattern of being taught and who teaches them.)

If you're particularly confident in your ability in a subject, you might consider talking your way around prerequisites. Perhaps you've taken one course in the area and found it too easy, so you want to move on to the upper-level courses. Or maybe there's a particularly good class being offered, but you lack the prerequisite. If you feel up to the challenge, go for it! Contact the professor teaching the course and explain your situation. Explain that you feel confident in what you know already, and in your ability to catch up quickly. Be sure to also tell him how much you want to take his class—flattery will get you everywhere. If he feels that you'll be lost, though, respect his opinion—he knows what you need to have covered to understand his class. Skipping prerequisites is risky, and we would only recommend it if you're very confident. Otherwise concentrate on finding the best classes at the level available to you.

Courses, Sections, and Selections

You might not always be able to choose which courses to take; sometimes you just have to fulfill your requirements and hope for the best. You can almost always choose your section, though.

Some classes may be taught several times during the same term. Each of these classes may be a section of the same course; for example, there might be five different professors teaching five different sections of one single course. Information about your section won't be reflected in your transcript—all anyone will see is that you've taken the course.

The way that a course can be divided into sections varies. Some courses have completely independent sections; that is, the professors are free to design their syllabi and exams as they please. (Sometimes the content is even entirely up to the professors, especially in humanities classes.) Other courses have one professor acting as coordinator, with the instructors following his syllabus exactly. Exams for these courses are often common; that is, all students take them, regardless of section. Sometimes all sections of a course attend a common lecture, and are only differentiated by recitations. The number of sections offered each semester depends on the enrollment in the course. At higher levels (see *course levels*) or in less popular classes, there is often only one section of the course available each semester.

It's worthwhile choosing your section carefully. For example, at our university there are always tons of sections of Calculus I—more than one hundred—and these sections are taught by different professors. Depending on the professor, students may breeze through the course or struggle, but none of this is reflected at the end of the day in a transcript. All that shows up there is the course and what the grade was. There is no way of telling if the professor was incredibly demanding or simply incapable of communicating the material. As always, picking the right professor is incredibly important.

Final Exams

Final exams transcend differences among colleges. As the end of the semester rolls around, students everywhere share the same stress. In many classes, your grade for the semester depends largely on this one exam. Grades in high school are usually based on continual assessment, so one poor exam is more easily averaged out. Finals in college are usually worth between 40 and 60 percent of your grade, and while we've taken classes that have no final, we've taken others that have nothing but a final.

Math and science classes are virtually guaranteed to have final exams, but some humanities courses may assign papers, projects, or take-home exams instead of an in-class exam. Aim to get these assignments done as early as possible. Once the exam period starts you'll want to be able to put your energy into studying—having finished up your other assignments gives you a terrific advantage.

Most universities offer students some time between the end of classes and the beginning of exams in which to study. This time can range from a day or two to a few weeks. You'll also find that you can squeeze in studying during the exam period when you don't have any scheduled exams. This stretch is the most intense of the semester, but it can be incredibly difficult to stay focused during it.

Here's an all-too-familiar scene. You've worked hard all term long; you read everything assigned and then some; you attended every class and visited office hours as problems cropped up. Frankly, now you're pooped and just can't wait until the break begins. But remember: you owe it to yourself not to blow the course at this stage just on account of fatigue. You need to catch a second wind, and jump back into the thick of things, recharged and refocused.

Your final provides you with a chance to pull everything you've learned into one cohesive whole. Look upon your finals period as an opportunity to put in the sort of effort that will let you own the material, as opposed merely to getting a good grade. Besides, if you don't give your best effort now, your grade won't reflect your overall achievement. You should aim to get to know the material well enough to remember it once the semester is over. Education is supposed to be progressive and cumulative; why move on to the next stage without doing what you can to make sure you've mastered the previous stage? Retaining the subject is obviously essential if the class is a prerequisite to other courses you want to take, but is still important even if it isn't. You'll still benefit in your other classes; the more you know, the better you'll do. The most disparate subjects can relate to each other—math in philosophy, philosophy in economics, and economics in real life. Remembering past subjects can give you a boost in unexpected places. Use your finals time as an opportunity to make this possible.

Grade Point Averages (GPAs)

Your grade point average is exactly what it says—it's the average of all your grades in all your courses. Many universities use a four-point scale, where an A corresponds to 4.0, a B to a 3.0, C to a 2.0, D to a 1.0, and F to a zero. Some other schools use a 5.0 scale, where A corresponds to 5.0 and so on. With this in mind, if you're asked for your GPA when applying to programs outside your college, mention the scale your school uses. (Unless, of course, you're on a 5.0 scale but wouldn't mind having your GPA interpreted on a 4.0 one.) Most schools also allow for fractions, for example, an A- or a B+ will fall somewhere between 3.0 and 4.0.

GPAs are not simple averages; your grades are weighted according to the number of credits the class is worth. This just means that a grade in, for example, a four-credit class will count four times as much as a grade in a one-credit class. For this reason, it's worth putting extra effort into classes that are worth a lot of credits.

Obviously, you want to get as high a grade point average as you can. Whether you can stay in your university will be determined by your GPA. People *do* get kicked out of school if their GPAs are low enough—we've both known too many people this has happened to. How low they can go varies from school to school, but you generally need to fail quite a lot of classes. Even if you aren't actually failing, though, you may not get credit for your major if you receive below, say, a C.

In the event that you do unfortunately fail a class, find out if your school allows you to retake failed classes. You may have the option to retake the class and replace the F with the grade you receive the second time around or at least the average of the two grades. A similar option may also be available if you can't get major credit from a class because the grade was too low.

If you realize near the beginning of the semester that there's a good chance you'll do very poorly in a class, consider withdrawing from it. Most schools let students withdraw from classes until about halfway through the semester. Withdrawing is different from dropping a class in that the class will still remain on your transcript with a W (for withdrawal) in place of a grade. As students usually withdraw from classes because they're doing badly in them, Ws carry a slight stigma (though administrators often tell you otherwise) and so should be avoided if possible. They are definitely preferable to Ds or Fs, though.

Lecture Halls, Classrooms, and Class Sizes

Class sizes can vary a lot within a single college and especially between different ones. We've had classes with as few as seven students (apparently Logic 408 isn't a popular course), and ones with over four hundred enrolled. A friend of ours once taught a course with over a thousand students. Obviously some rooms are better equipped to deal with classes of this size than others; those huge, stadiumlike halls (complete with amplification) are referred to as lecture halls, in contrast to the smaller classrooms that are more reminiscent of high school. The distinction between the rooms isn't too important, but the difference between the class sizes is.

The majority of people learn better in smaller, more intimate environments. It's certainly a lot easier to get lost in the anonymity of the giant lecture hall. Indeed, it's a well-known fact that students feel more comfortable about missing classes the larger the class size is.

While some courses are only ever taught to large classes, don't assume this is necessarily the case for your classes. Sometimes departments offer smaller (and relatively unpublicized) versions of large courses. Contact the department to see if there is any such alternative available, and don't be put off if the alternative is intended to be more advanced or faster paced than the regular sections. Smaller classes allow for more individual attention, which can offset a faster pace and let you learn even more. (More than once we've also seen these smaller sections end up being *less* work than the big ones.)

If your department doesn't have any alternatives to the large classes, don't despair. The strategies in this book will show you how to seek out the individualized attention you may need even in the biggest of lecture halls. The course may also have a recitation in which you get to be with a smaller group of students to review material from the lecture. Recitations are often run by graduate students—who may be good teachers themselves—but don't bypass the advantages of getting to know full professors rather than grad students. This is more difficult in big lecture halls, but is still quite possible.

Majors and Minors

Virtually every college requires its students to declare a major in order to graduate. Majors are usually chosen and declared at some point during sophomore year, though some schools ask for them toward the end of freshman year. (A few schools even ask students to declare their majors when they apply.) With your school's deadlines in mind, we recommend taking as much time as you can before actually declaring. You have nothing to gain by rushing into anything, and it's important to be sure about your choice.

The majors on offer to you depend on your school. Unless your college is a specialized institution (e.g., one devoted to engineering or fine arts), you should have a wide range of subjects to choose from. The single most important factor in choosing a major is whether it interests you. If your major bores you, you'll spend the next four years taking classes you won't enjoy and that you'll ultimately resent. Far too many students we know just don't like their majors and are enjoying college a lot less as a result.

Some students enter college having already decided on their majors, and others have no idea. Even if you think you know what you want to study, make a point of trying other classes during your first year. There are courses and probably entire fields that you know nothing about, and that might turn out to be very interesting. Look at it this way: after your undergrad years are done, you'll never have the chance to learn about so many different topics again. Don't decide in advance that you want to study X and X alone.

Many schools require that students carry a minor in addition to a major. Minors require less than half the number of classes that majors do, so are much less time-consuming. In most cases, your choices for minors will be the same as for majors. If you find you like your minor a lot, find out if your school allows you to double major. Majors require varying numbers of courses, so double majoring may not be feasible if both majors are very demanding. If you're interested in more than one subject, though, a double major is definitely worth considering.

Registration

At some point before the semester begins students have to register for their classes. At some institutions, this happens months before the new semester starts—in the middle of the previous semester, say—while at others, students might have to wait as late as until a few days before classes begin. Almost all colleges have incoming freshmen register separately from upperclassmen, a process called preregistration.

Preregistration usually happens during freshman orientation, when incoming freshmen are bombarded with information about the school they'll soon be attending. During preregistration, freshmen are often offered a limited selection of courses to choose from, and they must register without any information about the times and availability of different sections (see below). There's not much they can do about this at the time, except recognize that there are far more options available than are presented. Preregistration closely resembles course choice in high school—so much so that many students (ourselves included) don't imagine that normal college registration can be so different.

Real registration begins with the course catalogue. Some colleges provide printed brochures, some electronic documents, some both. This catalogue lists the courses being taught, the sections and their times, and usually the professor teaching the section. Think of the course catalogue as your registration bible. Study it carefully before deciding on your classes—there may be classes available that you'd never expect and that may well pique your interest.

The course catalogue should include the dates for registration—if it doesn't, find them out elsewhere by asking a faculty advisor or contacting your school's academic services. At most universities, classes fill up quickly. Missing the registration dates can leave you shut out of the courses you want to take.

The dates at which students can begin to register usually depend on class year or number of credits. Thus, while seniors have no trouble with closed sections (see below), this can be a big issue for freshmen. If your school has its registration dates based on number of credits, bear in mind the benefits of moving your registration date up a day. If the difference between registering on Monday versus Tuesday is only about a course-worth of credits, consider taking an extra (easy!) course so that the next time registration rolls around, you're a day ahead of most of your year group. Advanced Placement credits from high school help here too, as they can add that critical number of credits.

To illustrate, our university has students with one credit register a day before students with no credits, and students with twenty credits register a day before students with fifteen. (The average credit load a semester here is fifteen.) Thus, freshmen entering with any credits at all have a huge advantage over those with none, and students who amass twenty credits over their first semester keep this advantage the next time they register.

But just how important is it to register as soon as possible? Sadly, at many institutions it's extremely important. Popular courses fill up rapidly, and the most convenient sections with the best professors are snapped up. Freshmen, even ones entering with many AP credits, often have a tough time getting into some classes. Sophomores too can have trouble, so it's worth your while to bear in mind the benefit of building up those extra credits to push your registration day up. By junior year registration is more relaxed, and seniors are sitting pretty.

Once your registration day rolls around, make sure you are among the first to register. Whether you have to register in person, over the phone, or online, prepare everything you need in advance and be ready to get started at the first opportunity. This might mean getting up horribly early—at our university, 6:30 a.m. But once you're registered, you can always go back to sleep and dream of the classes you're going to take. (Being fully conscious is also a plus—partying till 6:30 and then trying to register over the phone can be kind of challenging, as one of us found out her freshman year.)

If classes are full when you register, make sure you register for something else. You can always drop it later on. It's a good idea to plan alternative classes while deciding what to take so you don't end up replacing Biology with Armenian 101 in the heat of the moment. Bear in mind that classes may open up again. You should have a period of time in which to add and drop classes—keep trying during that time in case a space opens up. Failing that, visit the first day of class and ask the professor if he can let you in.

The add/drop period is very valuable, especially to incoming freshmen, though few realize it. Despite your having to preregister without much information about classes, your university may still have an add/drop period open to you. Get hold of the course catalogue for the semester and poke around in it. Maybe there's a better section for a course you're taking, or even a class or two that you weren't even aware of when you preregistered. Take advantage of this period—most of your classmates won't.

Requirements

Every college has its core of required courses. Some schools have only a few requirements outside of the major, while other schools have about enough to occupy the first two years. If your college has a specific orientation (e.g., engineering or music), its core requirements will reflect this. (If your college's core requirements are very time-consuming and of no interest to you, you might just be at the wrong school. One of us almost ended up at a school with about six courses' worth of literature requirements—which would have been quite painful considering her lack of interest in the subject.)

There's a distinction between core requirements and major requirements. Your major (and minor) will have a long list of requirements that you have to fulfill to graduate with a degree in that area. Your college's core requirements are ones that must be met before you can graduate, period. For example, you might need to take up to a certain level of math courses in order to graduate, regardless of your major.

Required courses are often the worst ones in the university, the typical example being freshman composition. Students across universities are compelled to take a course in writing their freshman year, a requirement that is universally hated. Required courses are often overenrolled, poorly taught, and uninspiring. Before you resign yourself to a miserable time, though, try and see if you can take the course with a better teacher or possibly even fulfill the requirement another way.

With all this in mind, it's best to get requirements over and done with as soon as possible. There's nothing to be gained in waiting to take them. Once your major is fully under way your time will be limited. Set yourself the goal of having all your core requirements done by the end of your sophomore year, so you have your last two years to focus on your major and any independent studies you might want to do.

It's incredibly important to figure out just what your requirements are. This sounds obvious, but every year seniors find themselves in danger of not graduating because they are missing core requirements. Get hold of a list of your college's requirements and decide how you plan to fulfill them. Some of the requirements will be general, that is, rather than taking a specific class you need only take a class in a certain discipline. These general requirements can often be fulfilled in creative ways—look for courses in the discipline that tie in with your interests. Once you've reviewed what you need to do, make an appointment to go over your plans with an academic advisor (see above). She can let you know if you're missing anything or if there are better options given your interests. Also, if you have any credits from Advanced Placement tests, find out from her if these credits can count toward your requirements—never just assume they either will or won't. It's not a bad idea to double-check your advisor's information in the undergraduate catalogue if you are at all unsure of her advice—university regulations change, and the average faculty member has a hard time keeping up with the details. Requirements are best dealt with early on and with planning. Nothing's worse than realizing senior year that you've overlooked some of them.

Study Groups

One side benefit of college is that it lets you to learn how to work cooperatively and productively in a group. There's a lot to be gained from this experience. If you're having difficulty in a course, one quick and immediate gain is that you can wind up in a study group with people who can explain the parts of the course you don't understand. Even if you're pretty much on top of the material, you can get an even better handle on it by explaining it to other people. Study groups are also like dress rehearsals for any cooperative projects you might have to do later on in the workplace—practice keeping your group on task and delegating parts of the work to various people.

Study groups seem to be formed more frequently in some disciplines rather than others, more so, for example, in physics and chemistry, less so in history or philosophy. There's actually no good reason for this divide. Humanities classes lend themselves just as easily to group work as the sciences do.

Selecting classmates to work with can be a tricky affair, but there are obvious do's and don't's:

✔ Don't choose to work with someone who obviously understands much less than you do.

✔ Don't choose to work with someone who will do all the work for the group.

✔ Don't choose to work with someone who is not interested in helping others.

✔ Don't choose to work with someone just because he or she is cute.

✔ Don't choose to work with someone simply because you knew him before the course.

✔ Don't choose to work with someone just because she happens to be sitting near you in class or lives in the same dorm.

✔ Do choose to work with someone because you recognize she has done well all term and seems to be committed to doing well and learning in this course.

✔ Do choose to work with someone who is reliable—someone who arrives and hands in assignments on time. (It helps the group to no end if the people actually show up.)

There are some obvious qualifications here. Prefer someone who actively participates in class discussion over someone who doesn't. Of course, we're talking about quality as well as quantity. Just because someone runs off at the mouth doesn't mean he knows what he's talking about. Listen to whether he's actually *saying* anything. The professor's reaction is also a good indicator of quality.

Once settled into a group, divide up the topics at your first meeting. Assign each person the lead role for some topic. Ideally, people should take the lead in the areas they're most comfortable with—people often have difficulty with different parts of the material. Keep in mind though that you are ultimately responsible for knowing the material by yourself; study groups are no substitute for individual work. Use them to come to understand the information better and to clear up confusion, but make sure you can still do the work by yourself once the session is over.

Tutoring

If you're having trouble in a class, tutoring can be a lifesaver. Although you can almost always find paid tutors (just look for advertisements around campus), colleges often make tutors available for free. These tutors are either paid by the university or are dedicated volunteers, so they usually do an outstanding job. Find out through an advisor or through older students whether your college offers a tutoring program like this. Perhaps there's a center where you can sign up to get help in various subjects.

If your college doesn't have such a center—or if it doesn't offer tutoring in the subject you need—don't give up hope! You might try asking your professor if he knows of a grad student or even an undergrad who could to help you. Grad students are often willing to tutor (although you'll probably have to pay them) and can be counted on to have a good handle on the material. You might also be able to pinpoint someone in your class who clearly understands the material very well and ask her if she's interested in tutoring. Given a choice between an undergraduate or graduate tutor, though, choose the grad student.

If your class happens to have a grad student doing the grading, find out if he'll tutor you. Not only can you be sure that he knows the material very well, you also gain by getting to know your grader, and you can be sure he'll take a little longer correcting your work if he's already invested in helping you.

About the Authors

Ernie Lepore is the director for the Center of Cognitive Science at Rutgers University, and is also a professor in the philosophy department.

At the time she coauthored this book, Sarah-Jane Leslie was a student in the Rutgers University Honors Program. She is currently a graduate student in the Ph.D. program in philosophy at Princeton University.